ANTHONY
JOSHUA

PORTRAIT OF A BOXING HERO

This edition published in 2018
by Sevenoaks an imprint of
the Carlton Publishing Group
20 Mortimer Street, London W1T 3JW

A CIP catalogue record for this book is
available from the British Library

ISBN 978-1-78177-865-4

Editorial Director: Martin Corteel
Design Manager: Luke Griffin
Designer: James Pople
Picture Research: Paul Langan
Production: Lisa Cook

Printed in Dubai

ANTHONY
JOSHUA

PORTRAIT OF A BOXING HERO

IAIN SPRAGG

SEVENOAKS

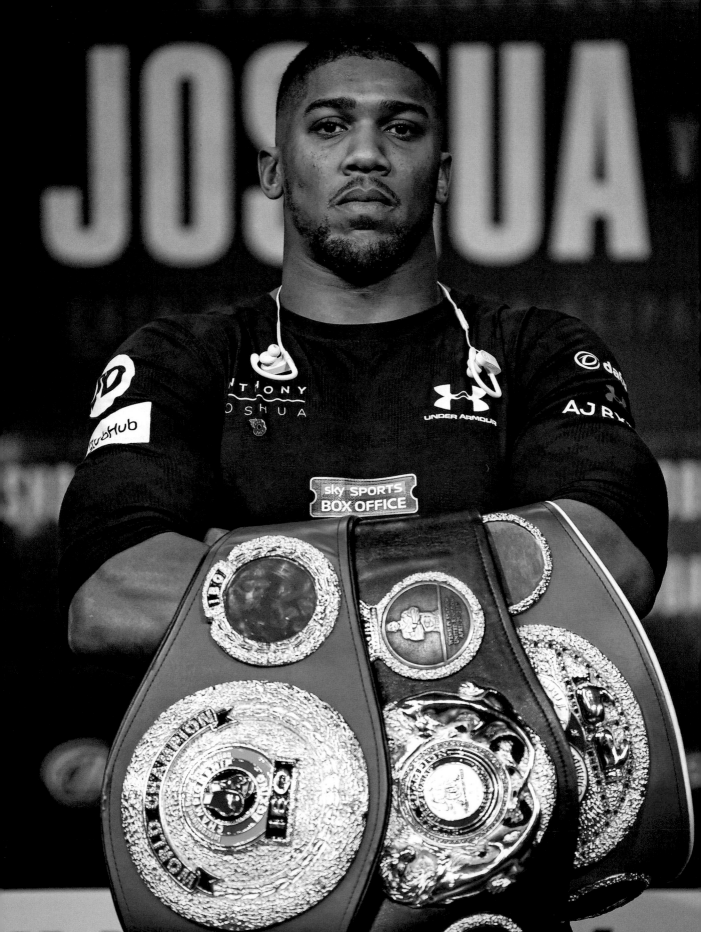

CONTENTS

s.Oliver
BLACK LABEL
StubHub
JDSPORTS.COM
williamhill.com
KLITSCHKO

CHAMPION
OF THE WORLD

Sport is nothing without superstars and in Anthony Oluwafemi Olaseni Joshua, boxing has unearthed one of the most explosive and charismatic fighters of any generation ever to grace the ring

OPPOSITE:
Anthony Joshua's journey to stardom began when the troubled teenager was introduced to Finchley Boxing Club in north London by his cousin Ben Ileyemi.

PREVIOUS PAGES:
Joshua's dramatic fight with Wladimir Klitschko at Wembley Stadium in April 2017 in front of a record 90,000 fans propelled him to the pinnacle of the heavyweight division.

British boxing has never been in ruder health. With seven reigning world champions at the end of 2017, the sport is enjoying a remarkable renaissance. But the undisputed jewel in the crown is Anthony Joshua, the man who has singlehandedly reignited an ailing global heavyweight division.

The ring's biggest and strongest exponents have always been boxing's marquee brand, but the division had become tired and predictable. Then AJ detonated onto the scene. After famously winning gold at the 2012 Summer Olympics in London, he decided to join the professional ranks and began rewriting the sport's record books. Joshua has now put heavyweight boxing back on the map.

At six foot six and weighing around 18 stone, he has a raw power coupled with a technical ability that belies his relatively late introduction to the sport, and which has seen him fight all challengers into submission in his still fledgling career. Few so far have been able to match his natural athleticism, speed and technique – and none have been able to find any answers to his sheer brute force.

His rise to greatness has been as meteoric as it has been merciless. His first pro fight came in late 2013 when he was just 24, and in less than three years he celebrated his first world belt after a trademark knockout of America's Charles Martin for the vacant IBF heavyweight title. AJ had reached the pinnacle of global boxing after only 16 outings.

That triumph was merely the appetizer. He has never made a secret of his ambition to become the undisputed world champion, and in 2017 he took another huge step towards making his dream a reality when he faced Wladimir Klitschko at Wembley.

Joshua had never before stepped into the ring with a man of the Ukrainian's quality. It was the chance of a lifetime, and AJ decisively seized it with both of his sizeable fists. After an epic 11-round battle, he added the WBA and IBO heavyweight belts to his burgeoning collection.

His spectacular victory propelled him into the sporting stratosphere and there are few more popular or famous athletes in the world today. Joshua has already transcended both boxing and his nationality and the only point of debate is exactly how much he can achieve in the ring.

His story is one of success in the face of childhood challenges. He was born in Watford in 1989 to Nigerian parents, and his brushes with the law suggested that the teenager would only ever make headlines for the wrong reasons. Family and fate intervened, however, to ensure his life took a dramatic, unexpected turn.

Finchley Amateur Boxing Club in north London was the scene for his Road to Damascus moment. Joshua was 18 when his cousin took him to the club – and from the moment he first pulled on a pair of gloves, he felt an immediate affinity with the sport. A new path now lay ahead of him.

AJ's first fight was held in late 2008 and within a year he had claimed his first tournament victory. Further amateur accolades quickly followed, but it was his Olympic displays in the ExCeL in east London in 2012 that propelled his career to a new level. From the moment he stood on the podium proudly clutching his gold medal after dethroning the defending champion Roberto Cammarelle, Britain had a new sporting icon.

The post-Games clamour for Joshua to go full time was loud and long, and ultimately proved irresistible. He signed for the renowned Matchroom Sport stable and rapidly built a reputation as one of the most fearsome and ferocious fighters on the circuit. It was simply impossible to ignore the youngster as yet another opponent was left crumpled on the canvas.

His first outing as a professional lasted less than three minutes. Subsequently, challenger after challenger was conclusively stopped in his tracks by Joshua's destructive punching power. Only one of his first ten fights went beyond the second round.

Blessed with an unerring work ethic, a humility born out of a tough background and all the athletic attributes a heavyweight could wish for, AJ now has history in his sights: he wants to become the first man ever to hold all five top weight world belts concurrently.

Only time will tell whether he is successful in his pursuit of all five, but Watford's favourite son can already be legitimately talked about in the same breath as some of boxing's all-time greats. His victory over Martin in 2013 to claim the IBF title made him only the fourth heavyweight in history to win a world title as the reigning Olympic champion. Those to have previously achieved the feat are the legends Floyd Patterson, Muhammad Ali and Leon Spinks. Joshua was also the first British boxer to hold the two coveted titles at the same time.

Boxing is undoubtedly an unforgiving sport, but it is also a form of show business – and AJ has proved to be pure box office. His showdown with Klitschko was broadcast live in more than 150 countries worldwide, and it broke the British record for pay-per-view subscriptions, set two years previously by Floyd Mayweather against Manny Pacquiao in America. Fight fans want to watch him because they know they'll be entertained while a legion of new supporters have been drawn to the sport by his huge personality and dynamic performances.

Joshua's career has already been a thrilling, rollercoaster ride but it seems certain there is so much more to come. The triple world champion will not turn 30 until late 2019 and with heavyweights renowned for their longevity, his best is surely yet to come. AJ is a man who has the world at his feet and a decade of unprecedented dominance in the division within his grasp.

1 **THE EARLY** YEARS

THE EARLY YEARS

Childhood upheaval and trouble with the police proved the making of AJ as he transformed himself from troubled teenager into a future world champion

There is a common theme in poetry and literature of inner strength forged in the crucible of adversity. In the case of Anthony Joshua, it's undoubtedly true that he would not be the fighter or man he is today were it not for his experiences in the first, sometimes chaotic 20 years of his life.

He is the son of Nigerian immigrants Yeta and Robert, who arrived in the UK in their early twenties, and he grew up on the Meriden Estate in the Watford suburb of Garston. At the age of five, his parents split up, and AJ and his three siblings were raised by their mother.

In 2002 his domestic situation changed dramatically when Yeta relocated the family to Nigeria and enrolled her then 11-year-old son at a boarding school. By his own admission it was a complete shock to his system – but while the school's regime was strict, he admits it wasn't all negative.

"I thought I was going to Nigeria on holiday. I wasn't prepared for it. At the time you think 'Why?', but as you get older you think it was good that you experienced it. We stayed out there, not long, only six months. [We started at] 5.30 in the morning: up, fetch your water. Your clothes had to be washed and ironed. We got beaten. That's my culture, beating."

He returned to England aged 12 and started at the Kings Langley School near Watford in Hertfordshire. It was here, in secondary education, that his natural athletic prowess, as well as his teenage tendency for trouble, began to emerge.

In Year Nine Joshua ran a phenomenal 11.6 seconds for the 100 metres and also played centre forward for the school football team. He was a gifted footballer, but his competitive edge led to problems: in one match the 16-year-old manhandled an opposition player by the neck and flung him onto the pitch, an act that resulted in a charge of Actual Bodily Harm (ABH).

"I was quite a good striker at school, but during one game this guy was trying to wind me up," he said. "I got him round the neck and threw him

over my shoulder. I didn't know my own strength and he didn't land too well. Incredibly, it went to court and I was charged with ABH. Luckily, they ended up giving me a slap across the wrist."

Sadly, further dealings with the judicial system were to follow. He left school at 16 and divided his time between sleeping in a series of hostels in Watford and staying with Yeta at the new family home in Golders Green, north London. The constant upheaval led, perhaps inevitably, to problems. After a late-night fracas in 2009, he was arrested and put on remand in Reading prison, for what he has subsequently described as "fighting and other crazy stuff".

His temporary detention terrified AJ to such an extent that he bought a set of weights in order to bulk up his muscles in readiness for the threats of violence which he believed would accompany a custodial sentence. In the end he was conditionally discharged, but the experience left a deep impression on the youngster.

"I was on remand in Reading for two weeks. There are idiots inside, and this is when you realize what you are dealing with in prison. Once you're there, it's fifty-fifty, because you've been found guilty, so I was preparing myself for the worst. It could have been 10 years."

After his release, Joshua moved back in with Yeta. He started work as a bricklayer, but it was his cousin Ben Ileyemi who was the most instrumental in helping him to start to turn his life around.

Salvation came in the shape of the Finchley Amateur Boxing Club.

ABOVE: AJ, father Robert (left) and aunt Cheryl (right) celebrate after his seventh round knockout of fellow Brit Dillian Whyte at the O2 Arena in December 2015.

Ileyemi was already at the club and he invited along the 18-year-old AJ, who was wearing the electronic tag that the court had ordered he have fitted. The teenager made quite an initial impression in the gym, and after a few sessions was soon pestering the Finchley coaches to allow him to graduate to the pads for the first time. They agreed, though it was a decision trainer Sean Murphy soon regretted.

"The thing with pad work is you do get problems with new boys," said fellow Finchley coach John Oliver. "They might hit on the edge of the pad and it bends your fingers. But not this boy who had come in. He hit the pad perfectly in the middle with one of his first shots, bang.

"Sean starts yelling and this big lad is following him, saying 'sorry, sorry'. We were all laughing, but then Sean has to go off to hospital, so that's a bit more serious. My god, when we hear back from him it turns out he hasn't broken his hand, he's shattered it. Every single metacarpal was smashed, maybe broken in 10 places.

"I've been in rooms with Muhammad Ali and Mike Tyson and I don't think I've ever heard something like that. Even now, Sean has problems with that hand. After one of those first sessions I told my partner that I had just seen a future world champion."

Murphy and Oliver were not the only ones made to sit up and take notice of Joshua in those early visits to Finchley. Spencer Oliver, the former European super-featherweight champion, was there the first night he came through the door with his cousin. The gym was run by Oliver's late father, who ran his expert eye over the teenager and was left in no doubt he was watching a star in the making.

"When he arrived I'm pretty sure he was on an ASBO at the time," Oliver said. "His physical presence stood out straightaway. Ben had brought him in purely to get him off the streets. Josh looked raw and strong and I can remember my dad saying that he is going to be special. But up to then, Josh really was living a bad life. It seems a cliché when we say boxing was a person's saving grace, but it really was in his case."

Joshua had been bitten by the boxing bug. Ileyemi lent him £25 to buy his first pair of boots and AJ quickly became an increasingly familiar face at the club. His love of the sport grew to such an extent that he lost his job as a bricklayer because he opted to travel to an annual tournament in Las Vegas with Finchley rather than heed his boss's dire warnings about an imminent P45. By now the ring had become his new home.

"[Ben] got me to come down to Finchley and it was a real workout," he said. "There were a group of super-heavyweights there, seven of them, so I got to progress pretty quickly, but they gave me a hard time at first. But it's about technique. I'd take silly shots. But I improved, I stuck with it."

The potential and sheer physical power AJ displayed came as no surprise to Ileyemi, who was already acutely aware just how dangerous his cousin could be.

"We used to scrap and I would get the better of him. Then things changed. We were messing around a couple of years ago and he hit me in the ribs. I never actually told him at the time, but I was in pain for about four days. Imagine taking a scaffolding pole and wrapping a pillowcase on the end, then getting whacked with it. That's what it is like."

For the next three years, Joshua would work his way rapidly up the amateur ranks, debuting competitively in the ring in 2008, but his story had one more almost disastrous twist when he once again found himself on the wrong side of the law.

In 2010, he was pulled over by the police for speeding in Colindale, north London. A search of his car uncovered eight ounces of cannabis and he was charged with possession and intent to supply a Class B drug. The maximum sentence for the offence is a 14-year prison sentence.

His future now hung in the balance. He had just broken into the British amateur boxing squad and many pundits were already tipping him to graduate to the professional ranks and win major titles. He had Olympic aspirations, with London 2012 on the horizon, and the 2011 AIBA World Boxing Championships were even closer at hand.

Joshua decided to plead guilty to the charges in the hope of drawing a line under the incident. The Crown Court accepted his plea and, rather than sending him to jail, sentenced him to a 12-month community order and 100 hours' unpaid work. He now had another entry on his criminal record, but he was at least free to continue his career.

"The arrest changed me a lot. It forced me to grow up and to respect my responsibilities. I'm not happy that I did what I did and there's no way that kind of thing will ever happen again, but in a way I'm glad it did because it woke me up. It was a learning curve for me. It was a sign for me to not hang around anywhere near the wrong people.

"I brought shame on myself and my family. It was really bad news for a lot of people who wanted to see me progress and I could see the pain it was putting my mum through. So I said to myself, 'This has got to stop.'"

He was temporarily suspended by GB Boxing in the wake of the court case, but Joshua's friends rallied round to ensure he made the most of his second chance. He returned to the gym at Finchley, and under the watchful eye of his trainers, focused once again on his training.

"Sean [Murphy] and I took him aside so many times to tell him to give up whatever he was doing out there," said Oliver. "That last one though was the real wake-up call. He was doing his community service in north Finchley, on an allotment next to my house. I used to sit with him in my car when he was done and talk about what he was doing with his life. The way he responded to what happened, I couldn't be prouder."

Joshua had come precariously close to throwing it all away. More by luck than judgement, he had twice avoided a prolonged spell in jail and he was now conscious there could be no repeat if he was to fulfil his boxing ambitions.

FOLLOWING PAGES:
Top left: Joshua's cousin and fellow boxer Ben Ileyemi.
Top right: Former European bantamweight champion Spencer Oliver was one of the first to recognize AJ's potential.
Bottom left: Trainer Sean Murphy took Joshua under his wing at Finchley Boxing Club.
Bottom right: Finchley coach John Oliver played a pivotal role in AJ's early development in the ring.

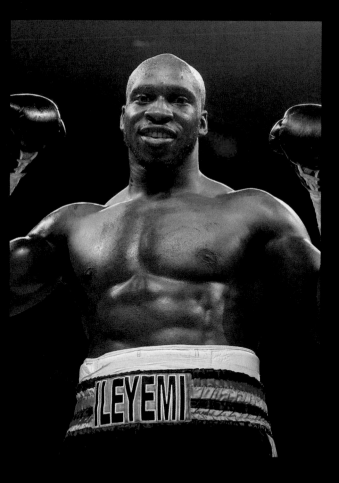

" My guardian angel decided I didn't need to be punished with a jail sentence. But I was on tag for over a year, and that helped. I became so disciplined when I was on tag. I would be at home by eight o'clock and because I had boxing, I lived the disciplined life. I started reading because I learned that so many champions educated themselves. Joe Louis, Mike Tyson, Bernard Hopkins. Before it was 'Act now, think later', but the discipline and reading changed me. **"**

ANTHONY JOSHUA on his 2█8 custodial reprieve

2 AMATEUR
CHAMPION

AMATEUR CHAMPION

It took AJ just two years to progress from his ring debut to winning his first major title in one of the most meteoric rises British boxing has ever witnessed

It was in late 2008 that Joshua made what was the short but surely nerve-wracking journey from the family flat in Golders Green to the cavernous upstairs room of the Boston Arms in Tufnell Park. The teenager was about to box competitively for the first time and it's not hard to imagine the apprehension he felt, waiting to enter the fray.

It's more difficult to guess how many in the small crowd that night, family and friends aside, had ever heard of AJ – but within three minutes the youngster had set a few tongues wagging. Not least *Boxing News* reporter Kerry Duffy, who was in north London that night to witness Joshua's impressive first round stoppage of his opponent.

"Not to be outdone by the preceding bouts, the seniors produced several thrilling displays. None more so than Finchley's Anthony Joshua, who on his debut left the ring to a new set of fans after stopping Minateur's Nathan Brede in the first round. The 18-year-old used his considerable 6'6" frame to maximum effect as he twice forced his man to a standing count before the referee came between them."

Joshua's amateur career was now up and running. Three more fights yielded three further wins, but in 2009 he returned to the Boston Arms to face the future WBC International heavyweight champion Dillian Whyte – and his development came to a painful halt.

The two fighters would renew acquaintances six years later in the slightly more salubrious surroundings of the O2 Arena, AJ winning by a knockout in the seventh round. In 2009, though, it was White on his debut who eventually edged an untidy, crude fight between two hugely inexperienced boxers. White won on points after three rounds while Joshua suffered the indignity of being put on his backside by his aggressive opponent.

"The fight was six years ago and I still watch it back," AJ said in 2016. "I last watched it three or four months ago. When I watch it I just think, what was I doing here, what was I doing there?"

The disappointment of his first defeat did not linger long. Later in 2009 Joshua competed at the renowned Haringey Box Cup, Europe's biggest amateur tournament, and claimed the super-heavyweight title to further underline his progress. Twelve months later, he successfully defended the belt in London. His points victory in the final over Swedish southpaw Otto Wallin is noteworthy because Wallin would go on to be drafted in as AJ's main sparring partner in early 2016, ahead of the IBF title fight against the American left-hander Charles Martin.

"The Haringey Box Cup is so important for your development as an amateur," Joshua said. "I was lucky enough to win it twice and it gave me a taster of what the big international tournaments are like. You have to make weight every day, you have to box up to three times in three days, often against a variety of styles and in front of a big crowd. It's a true representation of the types of competitions you'll be experiencing at a later stage of your career and an experience you'd be hard pushed to replicate."

The Haringey Box Cup was not his only triumph of 2010, however. Early in the year he headed to the ABA Championships at London's York Hall and made it through to the final. Then, in what was still only the eighteenth fight of his fledgling career, he beat the Isle of Wight's Dominic Winrow to take the title.

" When I turned down the offer of becoming a professional after winning the ABA Championships in 2010 I said, 'I didn't take up the sport for money, I wanted to win medals'. "

AJ reflects on his York Hall triumph

ABOVE: Joshua's powerful displays for GB Boxing during the AIBA World Boxing Championships in Azerbaijan in 2011 announced the arrival of the youngster on the global stage.

The win was significant for two reasons. Firstly, it meant AJ had now joined an exclusive cast list. ABA super-heavyweight champions of previous years include Audley Harrison, fellow Finchley graduate Dereck Chisora, David Price and Tyson Fury – all of whom went on to win Olympic and Commonwealth Games medals and, in the case of Fury, the world heavyweight title.

Secondly, his success attracted the attention of promoters. In the wake of his victory over Winrow, the teenager was offered £50,000 to join the professional ranks. Relinquishing his amateur status at such a young age was not part of the master plan, though, and although he did agonize, he eventually rejected the approach.

"I didn't take up the sport for money, I wanted to win medals. Not turning pro when I was younger is the biggest decision I've made. People were advising me to do certain things, but I followed my gut. You follow your gut and hope it works. The iron was hot, so do I do a deal or do I turn it down and maybe go out at the weekend on a motorbike and break my hand?"

Mercifully both his hands remained unscathed, and later in 2010 he added another belt to his burgeoning collection when he beat Amin Isa to become the Great Britain champion. AJ's elevation from unknown hopeful to the status of a bona fides prospect was gathering pace, and in 2011 he applied his foot to the career accelerator.

It was the busiest year of his career to date. Outside the ring he was dealing with the ongoing legal repercussions of his drugs arrest. When his GB Boxing suspension was eventually lifted, he set about making up for lost time.

His first major assignment came in May, when he defended his ABA super-heavyweight title at Charter Hall in Colchester. He faced Fayz Abbas in the final and although the eventual 24:15 points decision went in his favour, it was a rusty performance lacking sparkle – which spoke volumes about the turbulence of previous months.

"There's a lot more to come," he admitted after the fight. "I cannot blame my opponent for how I boxed, and that was not the real Anthony Joshua in there. This wasn't my best performance, you cannot judge me on that. I'm learning so much every time I fight. The World Championships is the big one this year and I just hope they have me written down as Number 1 on their notepad. I'm taking it one step at a time, I got this fight out the way, and now I'll turn my attention to the next thing. I'll be back in the gym on Monday. There is so much more to come, though. Boxing is my future."

Selection for the European rather than World Championships was, however, Joshua's more pressing concern in the wake of his second ABA triumph. It was not until the eleventh hour that GB Boxing made contact to confirm he was going to Turkey for the tournament. The late notice afforded him just three weeks' worth of training and he headed to Ankara for the biggest competition of his career in far from ideal shape.

It was to his credit that he was able to despatch both Eric Brechlin of Germany and Northern Ireland's Cathal McMonagle in the early rounds, but he was stopped by Romanian southpaw Mihai Nistor in the quarter-finals to end his medal hopes. Nistor remains the only fighter ever to have stopped Joshua in either the amateur or professional ranks.

The Romanian national champion came at Joshua relentlessly from the first bell. His aggressive, agricultural style unsettled his opponent, but it was not until the third round that the southpaw made meaningful contact, catching AJ with two swinging shots with his left. Neither rocked him unduly, but after his second standing count, the referee decided the fight was over. The look on AJ's face, a mixture of disgust and disbelief, told the audience exactly what he thought of the decision.

There was, though, a silver lining to the Ankara cloud. GB Boxing decided that AJ had done enough to earn his place in the team to compete in the upcoming World Championships in Azerbaijan, and for this he would now have the luxury of time to prepare. The stage was set for Joshua's first appearance on a global stage.

In truth, he jetted out to Heydar Aliyev Sports and Exhibition Complex in Baku in October as a quantity unknown to the vast majority of his rival super-heavyweights. News of his exploits in Britain had not yet reached further afield, his name was not high on anyone's list of pre-tournament contenders and he was certainly not among the Top 10 seeds going into the competition. AJ was supposed to be there first and foremost to gain valuable international experience.

His first three fights – against Tariq Abdul-Haqq of Trinidad and Tobago, Juan Isidro Hiracheta of Mexico and Mohamed Arjaoui of Morocco – all went AJ's way, but his quarter-final opponent was the renowned Roberto Cammarelle, the Italian two-time world champion, reigning Olympic gold medallist (from Beijing 2008) and the boxer ranked No. 1 in the tournament. Joshua had surely met his match.

The fight initially went according to the preordained script, Cammarelle dominating the first round. Then a left uppercut in the second and long right in the third from the younger man rocked the Italian. It was down to the judges to separate the pair, and they came back with a 15-13 decision to Joshua. The youngster had never overcome a fighter with such a pedigree.

"I always believed I could beat Cammarelle, so I'm not shocked about the result," he said. "It's not always the name but who is the best boxer on the day. Cammarelle is a legend and I have great respect for him."

The semi-final against Germany's Erik Pfeifer was a shorter and altogether more brutal affair. Joshua caught his opponent with a booming punch in the first round, and as blood flowed from Pfeifer's nose, the referee had no option but to call a premature halt to proceedings.

His foe in the final was Azerbaijan's Mahommedrasul Majidov, fighting in front of a partisan home crowd. The ensuing battle between the World No. 2 and the 21-year-Englishman proved to be epic. Joshua's jab gave him the ascendency in the first round, but as the bout unfolded, Majidov rallied and the fight became more of a brawl. AJ had to take a standing count in the second, and as the pair continued to go toe to toe, there was nothing to choose between them. When the bell sounded at the end of the third, the result remained in doubt. The judges deliberated and finally decided Majidov had edged it by the narrowest of margins, awarding the fight 22:21 to the Azerbaijani.

"I'm so disappointed," Joshua said after collecting his silver medal. "One hundred per cent I'm disappointed, I wanted to get the gold. You just asking me now, it hurts, man, it hurts. It's always one fight at a time, but we'd prepared well for the World Championships."

His disappointment was palpable, but while he was contemplating what might have been, others in Baku had watched his fights and come to rather different conclusions about his performances and what the future held.

"Joshua's emergence here has been a revelation," wrote the respected boxing journalist Gareth A. Davies in the *Daily Telegraph*. "The Finchley boxer, who turns 22 next week, stopped Pfeifer in the opening round of the semi-final, the referee unhappy about the blood pouring from the

> ## Losing to Majidov was a tough fight. But I knew I had to fight to the end, until that final bell. I know that if I keep on fighting, right until that bell, I'm going be fine. That's how I get through. **"**

AJ on being denied gold

FOLLOWING PAGES:
AJ listens intently to the speeches at the Aviva and *Daily Telegraph* School Awards at Twickenham Stadium.

German's nose. Joshua had already shown in the opening two minutes that he possesses poise, power and movement, and his booming shots looked to have broken Pfeifer's nose.

"It has been a remarkable tournament for Joshua, signalled notably with a win over Roberto Cammarelle, the Olympic and two-time world champion, at the quarter-final stage. After those nine minutes, Joshua became a commodity whose stock will rise as far as the professional ranks after next year's London Games. A massive learning curve for Joshua. A star is born."

Prophetic words indeed – and ones with which Davies's press colleagues evidently agreed. The Boxing Writers Club of Great Britain named AJ as their Amateur Boxer of the Year for 2011. Less than three years after his maiden fight, the boy from Watford was beginning to make serious waves.

More welcome recognition was quick to follow when he was invited to live and train four days a week with the rest of the GB squad at the English Institute of Sport in Sheffield. His victory over Cammarelle in the last eight in Azerbaijan had booked his place at the 2012 Olympics in London, and GB Boxing were keen to bring their embryonic star firmly into the fold. In 10 months' time he would repay the faith shown in him in truly spectacular style.

Only one British boxer had ever claimed super-heavyweight gold at the Games previously – Audley Harrison in Sydney in 2000 – and AJ was now on the path to emulating his achievement.

" Straightaway you could see all his physical advantages, but there was something about him too. A presence. In the ring, he was tall and rangy, and it was all about harnessing his attributes and steering him. AJ soaked up anything we could teach him. He was very dedicated – first in, last out. He was stimulated by it all and soaked up the details we could give him like a sponge. He listened to everyone. **"**

RICHIE WOODHALL, Team GB technical adviser, on AJ's first appearance at the English Institute of Sport in Sheffield

3 | **OLYMPIC** GLORY

OLYMPIC GLORY

With his Team GB place at the 2012 Summer Olympics in London now assured, Joshua set his sights on making his mark on amateur boxing's greatest stage

It is a rare breed of boxer indeed who is fortunate enough to compete at the Olympics, let alone stand on the podium clutching a medal. The Games are the pinnacle for the amateur ranks of the sport, and over the years some of Britain's most iconic fighters – from Henry Cooper to Amir Khan, Alan Minter to James DeGale – have represented the country with distinction at the Games.

Joshua joined their ranks courtesy of his quarter-final victory over Roberto Cammarelle in Azerbaijan in 2011, but with less than a year in which to prepare for the biggest challenge of his career so far, there was no time to waste. The youngster needed to be in the best shape of his life. With his personal problems well and truly behind him, he worked tirelessly with the Team GB coaching staff in Sheffield.

He would go on to do Britain proud, but a fascinating footnote in the Joshua story is the intriguing if unconfirmed report that he could potentially have boxed for Nigeria, his parents' home country, at the 2008 Summer Olympics in Beijing.

The man himself has never commented on the rumour, but it seems that the youngster's Olympic career could have unfolded rather differently. At least, that's the story from Obisia Nwankpa, the former Commonwealth light welterweight champion between 1979 and 1983 and the head coach of the Nigerian national team at the time.

"He reached out to us, asking to be part of our Olympic team [in 2008]. So we invited him to come down and take part in trials. Unfortunately he did not appear when we asked him to and came down only when we had finished our trials, finalized our team and were about to travel for a training tour. Maybe other coaches would have accepted it, but I could not. It's a pity he did not get his chance at that time, but the two boxers we selected then were outstanding and experienced and there was no way I was going to drop them for somebody I had not even seen."

Whatever the truth, AJ did not box for Nigeria in 2008 and their loss was to be Britain's glorious gain. In the build-up to the London Games, there was absolutely no doubting exactly where his allegiance lay.

"I'm very proud to represent Britain," he said. "If you win an Olympic gold, you are never a former Olympian. As a professional, as a heavyweight champion, once you lose the belts you are a former heavyweight champion. But you are always an Olympian, you can't take that away. Boxing at the Olympics is on my mind every day. I want to get the gold medal at those Olympics."

The comparisons between AJ and Audley Harrison, the super-heavyweight champion in Sydney 12 years earlier, were perhaps inevitable as the Games approached, and Joshua readily acknowledged the impact Harrison had made on the domestic amateur ranks.

"A lot of people have got bad things to say about him but at the same time, for British boxing, he opened up so many gates. He was an ABA champion, a Commonwealth champion, so as an amateur you've got to remember what he did. I know he didn't do too well as a pro, but from an amateur stance, he's an Olympic champion as a boxer and he is British."

Joshua's selection for the Games would have a pivotal effect on his subsequent career in more ways than one – not least because it brought him into regular contact with Rob McCracken. Team GB's head coach would help steer the youngster through his Olympic odyssey and, in recent

ABOVE: AJ outside the Olympic Stadium with fellow Team GB boxers (left to right) Andrew Selby, Fred Evans, AJ, Tom Stalker and Luke Campbell, ahead of the Games which would propel him to fame and ultimately the professional ranks.

years, the perils and pitfalls of the professional ranks. In 2012, however, the former Commonwealth middleweight champion was focused solely on ensuring AJ was ready for London.

"We always knew we had something special on our hands with Anthony, but his rate of progress this year, for someone who is still relatively inexperienced, has been absolutely fantastic," McCracken said. "As long as he continues to work hard in the gym, listen to the coaches and develop as a boxer, then he has every chance of being a star in his hometown Olympics."

By the time the boxing events at the Games finally arrived in August 2012, Joshua stood fourth in the world rankings. Fifteen of the sport's finest amateur super-heavyweights were waiting for him, however, and even with a vociferous, partisan home crowd cheering him on inside the ExCeL, the jury was still out. Did he really have what it takes to secure a medal?

BELOW: Joshua took time out from his Olympic preparations to spar with Hollywood actor Will Smith, the star of the 2001 Muhammad Ali biopic.

OPPOSITE: AJ was aiming to become only the second British boxer, after Audley Harrison at Sydney 2000, to be crowned Olympic super-heavyweight champion.

His first, round-of-16 fight was against Erislandy Savón of Cuba, the nephew of the renowned three-times Olympic heavyweight champion Félix Savón. The pundits widely agreed that this would be a tough opening bout, and those pre-fight predictions were borne out.

The Brit entered the ring to predictably deafening cheers, but as the fight unfolded, it was clear that Joshua was up against an opponent of real quality and technique. The atmosphere gradually became more muted as Savón evaded much of what Joshua threw at him. The Cuban's speed made him an elusive target and when the bell sounded at the end of the third round, no one inside the ExCeL was sure which way the decision would go. The 10 judges gave it 17-16 to the Brit. So, despite the experience of an at times uncomfortable examination of his credentials, AJ was safely through to the quarter-finals five days later.

"I knew it was a close fight and I leave these things to the judges. I had the crowd against me in the World Championships in Baku when I lost the final. He was much more slippery than I expected. I must put it behind me and move on."

More danger lay in wait in the last eight in the shape of China's Zhang Zhilei, an Olympic silver medallist in Beijing four years earlier. Victory would guarantee Joshua at least a bronze medal and in his second appearance at the Games, he came out in altogether more convincing fashion.

He took the first round comfortably on points, but it was in the second that he underlined his superiority over the Chinese, flooring

" I'm lucky to have this one-off chance and I'm doing everything in my power to seize it. For nearly all of the greats, winning an Olympic gold was a stepping stone to incredible careers. "

JOSHUA looks ahead to London 2012

his opponent with a booming right hook. Zhilei recovered to share the spoils in the third, but it was too little, too late: the judges scored it 15-11 to the home favourite.

'I'm glad I've got the medal, but I want to go all the way. Every fight is a learning curve for me and Lennox [Lewis] has advised me to use my jab more. I also know I must keep my feet on the ground. That's what a medal represents – it's the journey, and it won't stop here. I'm just going to get tougher."

There were just four days in which to rest and recuperate before his semi-final. His opponent was the imposing Kazakhstan fighter Ivan Dychko, and Joshua was under no illusions that the hard-hitting southpaw would ask significant questions. Standing at six foot nine, Dychko had the height advantage, and he had marched into the last four in London following two landslide victories in the earlier rounds.

The early exchanges witnessed little to separate the two men, who finished the first round four points apiece. The second was a repeat performance and as the final three minutes beckoned, the pair were deadlocked at eight points each. It was now or never for AJ if he was to keep his dream of Olympic gold alive. He responded magnificently, a superbly directed right shot drawing blood from Dychko's nose. The crowd

ABOVE: AJ, in blue, began his bid for Olympic gold at the ExCeL with a hard-fought and narrow points win over Cuba's Erislandy Savón.

roared, Joshua stepped up his work rate, and courtesy of the judge's 13-11 decision in his favour, he was through to the final.

"I have just got to stay calm," he told reporters after the fight. "That's all I keep telling myself. I'm still a day away from gold. It is not just about me. I know I have got my family at home, my coaches at Finchley ABC, the friends up there and everyone buzzing. It's a team achievement and I am just happy I can make everyone smile."

His date with destiny was 12 August 2012 and his rival for the title a familiar one: Roberto Cammarelle, the reigning Olympic champion and the man he had beaten in the quarter-finals of the World Championships a year earlier. The Italian did not let the word revenge pass his lips in the build-up to the fight, but there was no doubt Cammarelle felt, at least

privately, that he had a point to prove. "He deserved to beat me in the world championships," he said. "This time I will beat him."

There were many who believed him. The Italian had the pedigree, after all, and he had proved his class in his own semi-final, beating on points the world champion Mahommedrasul Majidov, who had overcome Joshua in Baku 10 months earlier. As befitted a final, the fight would be AJ's greatest challenge yet.

A certain Wladimir Klitschko was in the audience at the ExCeL to witness proceedings. The Ukrainian had won Olympic gold at the Atlanta Games in 1996, and the reigning WBO and WBC world heavyweight champion now sat down to watch the nine minutes that would decide the 2012 champion. It was time for the action.

The first of the three rounds saw the home favourite make light of the magnitude of the occasion with a series of penetrating jabs, but his concentration lapsed in the final seconds of the opener and he was caught in the corner. Cammarelle's late burst allowed the Italian to steal the round 6-5.

Joshua rallied in the second with another series of successful jabs, but Cammarelle was nonetheless getting through with punches of his own. The juddering left hook from Joshua was undeniably the shot of the round, but the Italian edged it with the judges and took the second 7-5.

The Brit was trailing 13-10 heading into the final three minutes, and it seemed that his challenge would come up agonizingly short. The last two minutes, though, saw Joshua display unerring accuracy just when it really mattered. Landing a rapid succession of shots, he dramatically levelled the scores at 18 each at the bell.

"Joshua, who was under pressure at the end of the first round and at the start of the second, found composure in a hurricane," wrote Kevin Mitchell in *The Guardian*. "Cammarelle, a Milanese policeman, has been a fine champion for a long time and briefly seemed on the verge of overwhelming an opponent who had had only 43 amateur bouts, losing three.

"The scores were level at 18-18 after nine minutes and went to countback – incorporating the scores of all five judges rather than just the median three – and Joshua had edged it by three points. That was not convincing enough for the Italians, who appealed. When the result of the short hearing was confirmed, the capacity audience, not for the first time over the past fortnight, filled the hall with the most heartfelt roar."

It was a shattering denouement to the Games for the Italian and his disappointment was palpable.

"I still don't know why – even with the same score – I was the one to lose," he said in the wake of defeat. "I thought they would see that I was superior in the fight. In Baku [last year] versus Joshua, I didn't lose. In Ankara, in the European Championship final against a Russian boxer, I did not lose. It's now been three years that I feel that the judges are against me. I don't know if my punch is invisible. I feel tired. I want to go home. Maybe I want to cry."

The emotions experienced by Joshua were in sharp contrast, of course. As he began to come to terms with being the new Olympic champion, the 22-year-old from Watford was already being talked about in boxing circles as a potential future world champion.

AJ, himself, was happy to leave that talk to others. Standing proudly on the podium, with the national anthem playing, he was content just to revel in what he had just achieved.

"Sunday is a holy day and I have been blessed. There are no easy fights in these Olympics. I have pulled it out of the bag and my heart is pumping with adrenaline. That medal represents my journey and the support from my team. It is much more than a gold medal, it is a life experience.

"I'm a warrior and I needed a big last round to get this medal round my neck, and I had it. This is a medal for everybody that has ever helped me and for everybody to start their own dream. I have had to overcome a lot of obstacles, but I never stopped dreaming of the Olympic medal. I played it over and over in my mind. It was a close fight and it has made me realize I need more experience at the top level."

It would not be until the following year that he finally decided whether his education would be furthered in the amateur or professional ranks. This would be perhaps the most difficult decision of his sporting life, but what was clear was that Joshua had now become one of boxing's biggest draws.

" I was in serious pain, but I just won't ever give up in there. I will keep pushing to the last bell. My legs and everything were killing me, but I just kept throwing punches, catching him with straight shots down the middle. I never panicked. Sometimes I wanted to stop, but my arms were just flying. My job is to do the fighting in the ring. The judges' job is to decide who the winner is. I've had close fights all over the world and I've lost a couple in my short career. I take it on the chin and I move on. **"**

JOSHUA after he overcame Roberto Cammarelle to win the London 2012 Olympic super-heavyweight gold medal

4 WEIGHING THE OPTIONS

With an Olympic super-heavyweight gold medal around his neck and the boxing world at his feet, the time had come for Joshua to decide where his future lay

The Olympic Movement prides itself on its Corinthian Spirit. The Games celebrate the achievements of amateurs, but there's an inescapable irony that in certain sports, particularly boxing, Olympic success is perceived as an automatic passport to the professional ranks.

Many certainly envisaged as much for Joshua following his victory over Roberto Cammarelle in the Olympic final. After all, he was young, articulate and charismatic. Now that he had confirmed his credentials on the biggest of stages, it was surely only a matter of time before he traded in his amateur status in return for a lucrative pay cheque.

That was undoubtedly the hope of some in the ExCeL audience who witnessed his gold medal performance. Richard Schaefer for one, the chief executive of Oscar De La Hoya's Golden Boy Promotions company. Leading British promoter Eddie Hearn for another, the managing director of Matchroom Sport. And a third in the person of Wladimir Klitschko, looking for a potential new recruit to his K2 Promotions venture, established with brother Vitali in 2003. The leading impresarios of the boxing world were all there to cast a professional eye over a new champion in action rather than to enjoy the spectacle. They knew he was genuine box office.

Everyone waited with bated breath for Joshua to confirm he had turned professional. A leading bookmaker slashed the odds on the news to 6/1 in anticipation of the announcement. Lennox Lewis publicly declared: "Josh has what it takes now to become the next heavyweight champion of the world." The speculation reached fever pitch.

Joshua himself had other ideas. While the world was singing his praises, he reacted to his Olympic success in characteristically low-key style, limiting his celebrations to the purchase of a £800 motorbike. Any tentative approaches from would-be promoters were politely but firmly rebuffed.

"It's not about money. The Lottery funding is more money than I've seen in my life, and my mum and I can pay our bills now. But it is about what is right for my development as a boxer.

"To leave the Great Britain setup just for money would be a big mistake. It's a great experience to be working with such great people, [the head coach] Robert McCracken and his team. I don't want to lose that just for a bit of money thrown in my face. I didn't grow up with loads of money. I learned to cope. I'm happy with life.

"My mum's a really grounded person, so is my dad. He works really hard. It's not like he's got a lot. It keeps my feet on the ground. These memories are priceless.

"I will stay in the amateurs as long as possible. Sometimes it's hard against fighters with more experience than I've got. I want to dominate everyone in the amateurs, become a world champion, become European champion. I'm learning at each tournament. The more tournaments I go to, the more I'll improve as a fighter."

Time was certainly on his side. Only 22 when he claimed Olympic gold, he was six years younger than the previous British Olympic champion Audley Harrison. After securing the gold medal in 2000 in Sydney, Harrison turned pro almost immediately. By contrast, Joshua was now the king of the ring in London, but the amateur World Championship title still eluded him.

ABOVE: Flanked by Nicola Adams (left) and Anthony Agogo, Olympic glory propelled AJ to sporting stardom but he was initially undecided whether to cash in on his hard-earned public profile and turn professional.

There was also the tantalizing prospect of defending his Olympic title in Rio de Janeiro in 2016. No boxer in the history of the Games had ever successfully retained his super-heavyweight crown – and were AJ to attempt it, he would still only be 26. The idea of fighting in Brazil evidently appealed.

"Rio is there, but I'm taking it fight by fight at the moment," he said. "If I don't perform, well, you know how hard the qualifying is. I've got to take it step by step. But if I go to Rio, I'm going with pure ambition, because being able to take what I learned in London would be unbelievable. At the time, London was more like a national championship, because everything happened so quickly. It's only now that I've had time to reflect on it. Rio would be crazy."

In the immediate aftermath of the Olympics, AJ was true to his word and had eyes only for the amateur ranks. "The situation is that Anthony is back in the gym with GB Boxing today," said his manager James Cook in September. "There have been no talks about turning professional. He's staying amateur. He's got a lot to learn and he's taking his time and there have been no talks with promoters and nothing has changed.

"I don't think he's even thinking about it. He genuinely wants to just get back in the gym and train. He's had 43 fights, that's the reality of it. He's very, very young and he doesn't want to make any rash decisions. He likes the GB set-up and the professionalism of the team around him and that's where he's at."

The following month, he announced he would return to the ring in December, but the appearance failed to materialize. Rather than seeing him fight, his fans watched him on TV in the BBC's *Superstars 2012*, the new incarnation of the channel's old multi-sport challenge programme. As befitted a man of such athletic powers, AJ walked away with the men's title after defeating fellow London Olympians such as triathlete Alistair Brownlee, double gold medallist Mo Farah and high jumper Robbie Grabarz.

He was back in the spotlight in February the following year when he headed to Buckingham Palace to receive his MBE from Prince Charles, but for the fight fraternity it was not royal recognition that had them gripped but what lay in his future. For the moment, AJ had resisted the lure of professionalism, a temptation that had persuaded so many fellow Olympic champions to abandon amateurism overnight. Even so, many pundits believed it was still a case of *when* and not *if* he followed in their footsteps.

In July 2013, the news finally broke that the 23-year-old was going pro. He had signed a three-year deal with Hearn's Matchroom Sport and

> **" Winning gold in 2012 satisfied my lust for medals. And Lennox [Lewis] thought it was best for me to turn professional. I'll be able to handle the pressure. This is because of what I learned as an Olympian. "**

AJ on his decision to sign with Matchroom

would make his bow as a professional fighter at the O2 Centre in London in October. There would be no fairytale defence of his Olympic title in Rio.

The decision was a blow to the amateur ranks, of course, but not entirely unexpected. Joshua was the sof Great Britain's boxers at London 2012 to cross the great divide, joining Olympic bantamweight champion Luke Campbell, middleweight bronze medallist Anthony Ogogo and lightweight Thomas Stalker as a full-time fighter.

"While we would have liked Anthony to stay for Rio 2016, his achievement in winning gold at London was something very special and we recognize his wish to pursue other opportunities and challenges," said British Amateur Boxing Association chief executive Matthew Holt. "Like others who have represented their country superbly in recent years, Anthony will remain part of the GB boxing family and he will always receive a warm welcome at our training facility in Sheffield."

Joshua's move to Matchroom was in no way a rushed decision. Arguably it came later than was sensible. As he faced the press for the first time as a professional, he spelled out how much detailed thought he had given to what would be a life-changing resolution. "I took time travelling to meet ex-champions and exchanged emails with world heavyweight champions and boxing fanatics alike before making my decision," he explained. "I also spoke with various promotion companies and hired lawyers to make sure that if I were to sign a professional contract I would never have to bring it out again to take anyone to court, as boxing is well known for fighters taking issue with their contracts.

"After a year of gaining wisdom, thinking and planning I finally spoke with my amateur coaches and decided I was going to sign a three-year promotional deal and make the step to the professional ranks. I'd like to thank Finchley ABC and GB Boxing – they have backed me all the way, taking me from complete novice to world Number and Olympic gold. They have given me the foundations to move into the professional ranks.

"Matchroom is the best place for me to go on the path I want to take. They've got a great stable of fighters and it's going to be great to box on Sky Sports."

The smile on Hearn's face as he unveiled his new fighter to the press was as wide as Joshua's shoulders. The deal was the culmination of a long and determined pursuit of his man, the promoter having successfully outmanoeuvred a host of rivals to secure AJ's all-important signature.

Hearn had first met Joshua at the English Institute of Sport in Sheffield while he was preparing with Team GB for the London Games. Hearn was in Sheffield with another of his boxers, the double world middleweight champion Carl Froch, but it soon became clear that the youngster from Watford warranted more than a passing glance. He hit the heavy bag so hard that Hearn was convinced he'd smashed it off its hinges. From that

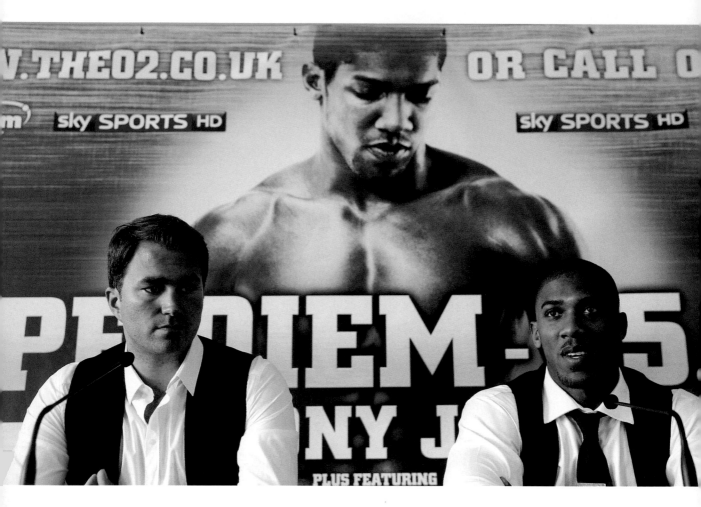

ABOVE: Joshua signed with Eddie Hearn and Matchroom Sport in the summer of 2013 as he embarked on his new career as a full-time fighter.

explosive moment, the boxer was firmly on Hearn's radar. Ten months after witnessing his Olympic glory, the promoter had his man.

"We don't want to put Anthony in with bums he can knock over, names people have never heard of," Hearn told the *Daily Telegraph*. "We are looking at Americans, and heavyweights who come to fight, not run away. The plan is to then have Anthony box on the undercard of Carl Froch's world title defence against George Groves.

"We talked about the future and I encouraged him to go and speak to everyone in boxing before we came to a decision. Sky Sports were very keen to showcase Anthony, as we at Matchroom Sport were. He is one of the most sought-after names in the sport already.

"Anthony is a great story not just for British boxing, but for British sport. He is young, talented, dedicated and can go on to become a role model in this sport. We believe if he is matched correctly and brought through in the right way, we are looking at a future heavyweight champion of the world."

With the ink on his new contract dry, it was time to bid farewell to those who had guided him at Finchley ABC and to the Team GB squad. He needed a full-time trainer to help him navigate the potentially choppy waters of his professional career. Matchroom had already arranged for a nutritionist, psychologist, physiotherapist and conditioner, but a new trainer was by far the most significant appointment.

He opted to work with Essex-based Tony Sims and train at his gym in Hainault. That meant he could continue in London rather than relocating. Sims was yet to guide a fighter all the way to a world title, but he had the experience and the ambition AJ wanted.

"As of next week I'll be with Tony on a daily basis," Joshua explained. "That's where I'm going to be. I'm ready to sacrifice anything if he wants me to. Lennox Lewis also gave me great words of advice. He's a great man. I read in the papers this morning people wondering is it going to be Lennox or Audley [Harrison] with Anthony Joshua, and really, the motivation for me is to make my own identity.

"I want to do it the traditional way and work my way up through the ranks. For me, it's not about money – it helps – but about athletic success. And that comes from hard work. Floyd Mayweather might look flashy, seem all about bravado, but behind the scenes, he's in the gym day in, day out. That'll be me."

Great things were inevitably expected of Joshua in his early fights in boxing circles, but Sims was in no rush to propel his charge to the pinnacle of the sport. His years of hard-earned experience told him that AJ, despite his Olympic gold, was still a work in progress.

"I think patience has a lot to do with being a top coach," Sims said. "You've got to be patient with kids. You can't expect kids to learn everything overnight. And also you've got to have experience as well. You've got to know when to push a fighter and when to hold him back. That's really important. I've found through working with a lot of different fighters over the years that the last week is really important. The week of the fight is important, when to push and when to hold back. Because you can overtrain fighters on the week of the fight.

"When I started out training, I had a few club-fighters. Looking back I probably never thought I was going to be in a good position, because there were so many big promoters in those days and I was just chucking my fighters on little, tiny shows at the Elephant and Castle, just club shows, dinner shows, average fighters. But I learned a lot in those days."

There were just three months for Joshua to prepare under the watchful eye of his new trainer for his first fight. He hadn't fought since his epic Olympic clash with Cammarelle in the ExCeL the previous year, and he now faced the considerable challenge of making his professional debut after a 14-month absence from the ring. The countdown to his new career had begun.

FOLLOWING PAGES: Even a tailored suit cannot camouflage AJ's impressive physique as he prepares for the press conference to announce he is turning professional.

" I had two distinct choices: either stay as an amateur and continue to learn and gain experience or turn pro and test the pressures of becoming the British heavyweight sensation and potentially being rushed through my career due to expectations based on my amateur pedigree. It took me almost a year to make the decision, a decision I can never go back on and a decision I feel I will never regret. I'm so determined and so willing to sacrifice anything and everything to achieve my dreams. **"**

ANTHONY JOSHUA on his decision to embrace professionalism

5 | STEPPING INTO THE UNKNOWN

Success as a full-time fighter has never been a fait accompli for even the most talented and decorated of amateur boxers. As AJ prepared for his professional debut, he knew it was just the start of a potentially long and punishing journey ahead of him

PREVIOUS PAGES: Joshua's triumphant debut fight in the paid ranks came in October 2013; it was his first foray into the ring since winning the Olympic Games gold medal the previous year.

OPPOSITE: AJ's eagerly anticipated maiden professional bout against Emanuele Leo of Italy at the O2 Arena in London lasted just two minutes and 47 seconds.

Close to midnight on 5 October 2013, Joshua finally stepped into the ring at London's O2 Arena. He was just 10 days short of his 24th birthday. As he emerged from the dressing room into the glare of the spotlights, accompanied by the sound of "Who Gon Stop Me" by Kanye West, his face could not fully disguise the nerves he was experiencing.

The fight – six rounds, three minutes each – was on the undercard of Scott Quigg's WBA super-bantamweight title defence against Cuba's Yoandris Salinas. The O2 was heaving and here, just five miles from the ExCeL and the scene of his Olympic triumph, AJ was about to embark on his new career. "Do we have another Lennox Lewis on our hands?" asked Sky Sports commentator Nick Halling as he entered the ring. It would not be long before AJ supplied at least a partial answer.

He revealed in the build-up to the fight that he received a good luck message from none other than Wladimir Klitschko. Whether he would need it against his opponent, Emanuele Leo of Italy, remained to be seen. Going into the contest, the 32-year-old boasted a decent record of eight wins from eight fights, three by knockout, but the calibre of his victims was debatable. What's more, in the last three years he had boxed only twice, and when the two men stood face to face in the ring, it was evident that the local boy was in far superior physical shape.

The bell for the first round was greeted by cheers from the crowd, and from the outset Joshua looked calm and focused. He immediately got his left jab working. Leo initially came forward bravely, but the debutant took complete control of proceedings, picking off the Italian with reassuring regularity.

“ I had to stay relaxed. There were big expectations on me as people wanted to see what I've been up to in the 14 months I've been away. Everyone will support me and let me crack on with it. Then you will **”** see the best of me.

AJ on his winning start as a professional fighter

Joshua remained patient despite his opponent's obvious, increasing discomfort. Then, 20 seconds from the end of the first round, he delivered the coup de grâce, unleashing a series of four quick-fire, short-range uppercuts with his right. Leo flailed wildly in a last act of disorientated defiance, but Joshua moved in to finish the job. As the referee rushed in to stop the fight and save Leo from further punishment, the Italian hit the canvas.

"He staggered Leo several times with right crosses and while the Italian marched forward gamely, the effect was rather like watching a World War One soldier walking into a battery of machine-gun fire," wrote Sean Ingle in the *Guardian*. "A series of concussive punches ended it two minutes and 47 seconds into the first round."

Mission accomplished!

OPPOSITE: Two days after despatching Emanuele Leo, Joshua was one of the star attractions at the 2013 Pride of Britain Awards in London.

BELOW: Three weeks after his pro debut, AJ despatched compatriot Paul Butlin in the second round of their fight at the Motorpoint Arena in Sheffield.

By any measure, this had not been a thorough examination of Joshua's professional credentials, but the explosive manner in which he had despatched his opponent so convincingly was nothing if not satisfying. Sterner tests would come, but for now AJ was content to enjoy the victory.

"This was just as important as winning the Olympics. I had been out of the ring for 14 months, but I've built a really strong team around me. It's going to be a tough road and hard work, but I'm going to put the work in. I'd love to be in the heavyweight mix, but I've got a long way to go to get there.

"We'll gauge my progress as I keep winning and keep learning in the gym, and we'll see what I am ready for fight by fight. I don't want to promise things I can't deliver. I don't want to talk much trash. I want to back things up. It's going to be a tough road and hard work, but I'm going to put the work in."

Three weeks later he was back in action on the undercard of Kell Brook's welterweight clash with Ukrainian Vyacheslav Senchenko. The venue was the Motorpoint Arena in the familiar surroundings of Sheffield, and his opponent the vastly experienced Paul Butlin, a British pro of 11 years' standing. At the age of 37, though, he was a fighter in the autumn of his career.

The opening round was a one-sided affair. Once again Joshua's jab looked in fine fettle, and he followed up with a series of muscular blows that rocked Butlin. The veteran had to fall back on all his battle-hardened years of experience to survive – and to ensure that, unlike the Leo fight, a second round was required.

Then, however, AJ needed only a further 50 seconds to bring a brutal end to the proceedings. A left hook saw Butlin's legs betray him, then a crunching straight right smashed through his defences, putting him on the canvas as well as opening up a cut above his left eye. Butlin bravely got to his feet, beating the count, but Joshua showed no mercy and stepped in with a succession of blows that forced the referee to stop the fight. The intervention came just seconds before Butlin's corner threw in the towel.

"He showed so much more composure tonight," said Eddie Hearn. "Butlin is a seasoned pro who went the distance twice with Dereck Chisora. This is a different class we are talking about right here. People talk about we've got to take him at the right pace, but that's going to be very difficult to do."

The brevity of the bout again left questions unanswered about Joshua's technique or his ability to take a decent punch. Butlin, though, was unequivocal: he made it clear that he believed the 24-year-old had more than enough raw power to go all the way.

"I've been in with the biggest lads in Europe. But Joshua's power is horrible. If he hits you, you're gone, simple as that. It's sickening, nobody hits harder than Anthony Joshua. The first jab he hit me with, I went back to the corner shaking my head. He caught me with an overhand right

that gave me nine stitches. How many heavyweights would have got up from the right hand Joshua hit me with? It was a horrible punch, the best I've taken."

With two commanding wins from two, Joshua had done all that could be asked of him. Even so, as he prepared to face Croat Hrvoje Kisicek at the York Hall back in London in November 2013, he admitted that trainer Tony Sims was not exactly getting carried away with his performances so far.

"The only thing I listen to about my prospects is what my coach tells me, and he tells me I'm rubbish and that I've a lot to work on. He tells me I have to keep my feet on the ground, that there are a lot of people out there who are better than me. That is why I need to keep on grafting in the gym. I do appreciate what people are saying about my prospects, but it's early doors. It's one step at a time and I have a long way to go."

Champions past and present, including former world heavyweight champion Larry Holmes and current British and Commonwealth title holder David Price, were ringside to watch Joshua fight in Bethnal Green. Kisicek's record of five wins and six losses was not one to strike fear into his opponent, and with the Croat surrendering a significant height and reach advantage, AJ was the clear favourite.

He did not disappoint the star-studded crowd. From the start he was on the front foot. His jab played the starring role in the first round, but it was a body shot that left the most lasting impression on Kisicek, who winced in pain. When the Croat desperately tried to counter, AJ stepped away from the danger with ease.

The second round was reminiscent of the Butlin fight. Joshua was in no mood for a protracted engagement and visibly upped the ante, catching his opponent with a left-right combination that sent him down. Kisicek took the count and found his feet at eight, but regained the vertical only to be welcomed by a further salvo of bruising shots. The outcome by now was inevitable, and midway through the round the referee Marcus McDonnell stepped in to spare the Croat any more damage. The fight had lasted 48 seconds longer than it took to dispose of Butlin.

"I worked on a few things in there," AJ said. "He was cagey, awkward and durable. It's important to work on things in the gym and take that to the ring. I'll be in Manchester next weekend performing again and I need to be ready for that."

His Manchester assignment was supposed to pit him against Argentina's Hector Alfredo Avila on the undercard of Carl Froch's defence of his WBA and IBF super-middleweight belts against George Groves. Fate had other ideas, though: AJ strained a bicep and on the advice of his medical team he was forced to withdraw. There was further frustrating news in December when a shoulder problem put paid to plans to face Welshman Dorian Darch at the ExCeL.

It was not how he had envisaged finishing 2013, his debut year as a professional. Still, there was the consolation of three muscular wins from three to show for his early efforts, and with the Darch bout rescheduled for February the following year, much to look forward to.

The fight was held at the Motorpoint Arena in Cardiff, and was to be Joshua's first professional foray outside England. Once again, he was expected to put his opponent away without undue alarm, though Darch's record of seven wins in nine outings suggested he might at least be a stubborn opponent. The Welshman, however, was under no illusions.

"I've got my limitations and I know I'm never going to be world champion. I also know Joshua is a huge guy and he's probably going to be too big for me. But you never know, I could hit him on the button and my world can change. It's hard as a heavyweight getting fights in Wales, so I told my manager that I was happy to take some risks. To be fair, he's come up with the Joshua fight and it's a massive opportunity for me."

The crowd in Cardiff was predictably partisan as the two men entered the ring, the majority of the cheers reserved for the Welshman. For most of the opening round, there was faint hope for the locals as Darch avoided his opponent's biggest shots and even caught the Englishman with a rare right hand. That proved a red rag to the bull, and AJ replied with a flurry of punches that was halted only by the bell.

The second round lasted less than a minute. A straight right visibly rocked Darch, and as Joshua moved forward purposefully, referee Terry O'Connor intervened. The Welshman looked poised to fall. It was a fourth straight win, but the first time the Olympic champion had failed to send his opponent to the floor.

"The Olympic gold medallist's seamless transition to the professional ranks continued on Saturday as he knocked out Dorian Darch in just two rounds in Cardiff," reported the *Daily Mail*. "The heavyweight was making his fourth professional outing and extended his 100 per cent record as he put his Welsh opponent down. Out of 24 rounds he could have boxed since joining the paid ranks, the 24-year-old has been in the ring for just seven of them."

AJ himself was unhappy with his performance, and acutely aware that his rise would not continue to be quite so meteoric if he didn't improve. His opponents were only going to get stronger, and he had to be prepared for significantly sterner challenges.

"Not too great tonight. A few things I was noticing in there when I was getting my jab going and my one-two, but you know how it is, the first round you are just warming into the fight. I was trying to capitalize on some of his weaknesses from early on, but as round two came along I started finding my rhythm. The next fight in March, hopefully you will see a bit of improvement."

OPPOSITE:
Welshman Dorian Darch became Joshua's fourth victim when he was stopped early in the second round at the Motorpoint Arena in Cardiff in February 2014.

FOLLOWING PAGES:
Anthony Joshua was a star guest at a press conference for the Robert De Niro/Sylvester Stallone movie *Grudge Match* at London's Dorchester Hotel in January 2014.

" I actually started alright. I was making him miss, which isn't something I normally do. I normally just go in there and have a bit of a scrap. For two-and-a-half minutes, I was making him miss and it was all OK. Then he caught me and my head was like a pinball. I didn't go there to lie down, but he was in a different league to me and you could tell that he lives in the gym. He was too good, too big and too strong and I hope he goes on to become a world champion one day. It would be nice to say that you've been beaten by a world champion. **"**

BRIAN DARCH *reflects on his defeat to AJ in Cardiff in 2014*

6 RISING THROUGH THE RANKS

RISING THROUGH
THE RANKS

Joshua's dream of a world title shot would ultimately only be realized by facing higher-quality fighters. In his next five assignments, Watford's favourite son took up the challenge in characteristically brutal style to claim the first belt

PREVIOUS PAGES:
AJ's impressive early displays as a pro saw him forge a growing reputation as one of the hardest-hitting heavyweights in the country – as Matt Skelton found out inside the first round in July 2014.

A quartet of bouts in only four months represented a frenetic introduction to the paid ranks for AJ, and there would be no rest in the wake of his victory in Cardiff.

Matchroom had already rescheduled his clash with Hector Alfredo Avila, which had been postponed because of Joshua's bicep injury. On 1 March 2014, exactly one month after fighting in Wales, he would step back into the ring against the Argentine in Glasgow.

No one was pretending Avila was a world-beater, but he was certainly durable. His record of 21 wins in 34 fights as a pro was testament to that. He had also made an impression on British boxing fans in early 2013, when he took Dereck Chisora, the former British and Commonwealth heavyweight champion, nine rounds at the Wembley Arena.

The build-up to the fight was as revealing as the action itself: Joshua entered the arena to the sound of "500 Miles" by Scottish band the Proclaimers. The audience assembled inside the Scottish Exhibition and Conference Centre in Glasgow loved it, and the choice of music demonstrated AJ's growing understanding of the professional game both in and out of the ring. He had learned that professional boxing was as much show business as sport.

What unfolded against Avila was as entertaining as the walk-on but did not last quite as long.

The first 90 seconds of the opening round were relatively uneventful as Joshua probed delicately with the jab. Avila managed to avoid any real punishment, but then, with 75 seconds left on the clock, the tempo suddenly increased as Joshua trapped his opponent on the ropes and

rained down a flurry of blows. The Argentine's only escape was a desperate embrace with the Brit. That proved only a temporary reprieve and once the referee had separated them, he was exposed again. AJ floored him immediately with a thunderbolt left. Avila writhed in obvious discomfort on the canvas, clutching his right ear, and the referee stopped the fight before he had even reached 10.

"There's definitely an improvement from my last fight, and that's what I was looking for," Joshua said after an evening's work that had lasted just 134 seconds. "It was clear to see there have been some improvements in me. As the opponents get better, we want to keep on doing that.

"When people are knocking guys out, there are always questions about whether they can go the distance. Everyone trains hard in the gym, but I think mentally I'm ready to go six, eight rounds. This is my last six-rounder and the opponents are going to get tougher. This is going to be an interesting year and there will be a time when you see me go past two rounds. I bet you I'll be fine."

ABOVE: Joshua made light work of Hector Avila when they fought in Glasgow in March 2014, knocking out the Argentinean inside the first round.

Boxing pundits probably gleaned more about Joshua's popularity with the public than they did about his potential in Glasgow that night, but Eddie Hearn was happy with the display despite the brevity of proceedings.

"He's progressing," Hearn said. "People will criticize the opponent, but Avila went nine rounds with Chisora. It's about showcasing Anthony Joshua all around the country. To see him walk out to that reception was incredible – that's why we love coming here so much. He's going all the way. We've got a problem in that I think he's ready for the division now. But we've got to keep progressing, keep learning. But right there, you've got something very special."

Three months later, AJ returned to the fray for his first fight at Wembley Stadium. The chance to box at the home of football came courtesy of the undercard of the rematch between Carl Froch and George Groves for the former's WBA and IBF super-middleweight belts. Such an iconic stage could only increase the 24-year-old's profile.

> **❝** I could see he was going to come out swinging straightaway. I knew he couldn't outwork me and I knew I'd break him down eventually. Potentially, I feel I could step up, but experience-wise, I haven't been more than two rounds yet as a pro. **❞**

JOSHUA reflects on victory over Matt Legg at Wembley

His opponent was 36-year-old Matt Legg. A record of seven wins in nine outings as a pro was unremarkable, and sadly for those who took to their seats early at Wembley to watch Joshua, he provided only fleeting resistance. To be exact, the fight lasted 83 seconds.

"None of Joshua's six opponents have yet taken him past two rounds but at least Legg, who entered the ring with a modest 7-2 record, gave it a go," wrote *The Guardian*'s Sean Ingle. "Having promised he would be 'sharper and faster than a lot of people expect' he attacked Joshua from the start with several swarming hooks. True, most of them caught thin air, or Joshua's gloves, but a couple did clatter home.

"Not that Joshua was overly ruffled. He bided his time, waited for Legg to expose his chin, and then shunted it backwards with a right uppercut that rocked him to his boots. A second venomous uppercut shortly afterwards – followed by a clipping left hook – finished him off."

The aforementioned second uppercut left a painful and lasting impression on Legg. "I got a broken eye socket. When I tried to get up, I couldn't even see. I had three months of nerve damage in the side of my face. For two months I had no feeling, it was numb.

"He's fast – people underestimate his speed. When he lets combinations go, he's super fast for 18 stone. It's amazing how fast his hands are. To walk out onto the Wembley pitch was like walking into the Coliseum as a Gladiator,

RIGHT: AJ took a break from the gym in the summer of 2014 when he attended Wimbledon with David Haye, the former WBA heavyweight champion.

OPPOSITE: Joshua's meteoric rise through the ranks continued after an explosive second round stoppage of former British champion Matt Skelton in Liverpool in July 2014.

especially when you're in with the new [Mike] Tyson. He hits you through your gloves, even when you've got your hands up protecting your head. The power of his punches goes through your gloves and there's nowhere to hide."

Liverpool's Echo Arena was selected as the venue for AJ's seventh fight in July 2014, facing compatriot Matt Skelton. At the age of 47, Skelton was undoubtedly at the wrong end of his career in the ring, though he had an impressive CV. At various times, he had held the British, Commonwealth and European heavyweight titles.

A former professional kickboxer, Skelton had become British champion a decade earlier when he knocked over Michael Sprott. That particular belt was very much on Joshua's mind as he discussed his upcoming challenge and the strides forward he was making in the professional game.

"I'm ready to take risks, but one step at a time, though, as this is a career. I'm not trying to run a 100-metre sprint. I'm on a marathon now, so next year will be interesting to see where we go, but I've really got to focus on Skelton, who should give me some problems.

"He's someone tall, rangy and a veteran of the sport. I haven't gone past two rounds yet, but it's early days and this is what I should be doing. Hopefully I will get another victory and then I think early next year it will be interesting to see where my management take me heading towards that British title, but what an honour it would be to fight for the British title."

The fight with Skelton on Merseyside initially followed the pattern of his previous outings. AJ established his superiority early on, but as the first round gave way to the second and the clock ticked, there was a growing possibility that Joshua would be taken into a third round for the first time.

It was not to be, however, thanks to the increasingly familiar power of his right hand. Skelton took a piledriver blow to the head, and hit the canvas. The veteran narrowly beat the subsequent count, but when he then toppled backwards towards the ropes, the referee intervened. With 27 seconds to the bell, the fight was over. It was a seventh successive victory for the Olympic champion after his longest stint in the ring so far.

"Matt was game, but the plan worked. I stuck to my jab. I'm learning all the time and, if I keep on progressing, I'll keep getting these first and second round knockouts. It's definitely a good name on the record, there's not much point in me fighting guys I'm knocking over all the time."

Defeat was the ninth of Skelton's pro career. It turned out to be his thirty-seventh and final assignment in the ring and in the aftermath of the fight, he acknowledged that his opponent's potency was not simply a product of Joshua's physicality.

"The funny thing is that it's not so much about power," he said. "Joshua is very accurate. He hits hard, don't get me wrong, but when it's combined with accuracy, that's hard to go against, isn't it? You can have a big, hard punch, but if it's not timed correctly, then it takes the sting out.

"I got the impression that you can't upset him. If you want to mix it up with him, get down and dirty, he'd bring the same back. In my eyes that's a good thing. I thought we would go the distance, but he was so much physically stronger than we thought. I can't take anything away from him and he looks like he could be a world champion with that strength."

The day after the contest, Eddie Hearn and Matchroom announced that AJ would next face Ukrainian Yaroslav Zavorotnyi in Dublin in August, but the fight never materialized. Instead his eighth opponent would be Germany's Konstantin Airich in Manchester in September. Before his return to the ring, the news broke that Joshua would box for a belt for the first time as a pro.

The vacant WBC International Heavyweight title was the prize on offer. It was a regional rather than truly global title, but it was a belt nonetheless. His rival would be Russia's Denis Bakhtov, and the two men would go head-to-head at the O2 Arena in London in October, just over a year after AJ's first fight as a professional. The chance to make his mark in boxing circles beyond Britain had come at breakneck speed for the 24-year-old, and some questioned whether he was ready for such a challenge.

That debate could wait, however, because the Airich bout was first on the agenda. Joshua ensured his preparation was faultless. He flew out to Austria to spend 10 days in camp sparring with and watching Wladimir Klitschko, who was at the time the triple IBF, WBA and WBO champion. It was an experience that left a significant impression on the youngster.

"I felt I belonged there, but Wladimir is different to everyone else," he told *Boxing News*. "He's been the champ for ten years, he's in a league of his own. For me to be where Wladimir Klitschko is there's a lot of work to be done. I can see myself potentially being there, but to own it and make it look easy, there's a little bit of work to be done. I feel I am talented enough to become the world champion, but to stay there for as long as he has, keep defending the titles and stay hungry for it, that's what I need to learn."

By mid-September, AJ was ready for the challenge of Airich, on the undercard of Scott Quigg's WBA super-bantamweight title defence. The 35-year-old Kazakh-born German heavyweight had fought 35 times as a pro, registering 21 wins. Interestingly, Airich had gone the distance in a defeat to Bakhtov just two months earlier. Most pundits still expected another Joshua victory, but with the WBC International title fight less than a month away the contest took on a greater resonance.

The opening round in Manchester's Phones 4u Arena was relatively unspectacular. Joshua seemed content to probe with the jab to keep Airich firmly on the back foot. Then, in the early stages of the second, the pace quickened as he unloaded a booming left hook that visibly rocked his opponent. He followed up with a big right and an aggressive combination that left the German sprawling on the ropes. It was only a matter of time before the referee was forced to step in and give Airich a standing count.

By his own post-fight admission, AJ thought it was all over at that stage, but Airich was a tough old nut to crack and he bravely soldiered on. When the bell signalling the end of the second round sounded, Joshua headed to his corner to contemplate the uncharted territory of the third round that awaited him.

If there was any anxiety on his part, it did not show and after just 40 seconds he unleashed a powerful flurry of blows that forced his opponent onto one knee to escape further punishment. Airich took the 10 count once again, but when he returned to the fray, AJ was in no mood for mercy and pinned him on the ropes, raining down more muscular shots. The German was on the canvas again, and this time the referee didn't even go through the motions of the count. Joshua had maintained his perfect professional record.

"I wanted to go eight rounds because he's durable," he said. "Some shots that I hit him with, some opponents that I've boxed, no disrespect, would have gone out in the second, but he stood up and took some good shots. But it's only a matter of time in boxing if you keep getting hit by big shots, and that's what I was doing, changing the angle, changing the power of my shots and I caught him with a peach of a punch."

The nature of his victory, albeit in the unfamiliar realm of a third round, was a timely confidence booster ahead of the showdown with Bakhtov. Hearn was certainly buoyant about AJ's prospects. "If you look at the progression of some of the great heavyweights, his is much faster. He's despatching people with ease every time. It's good to see him make bigger steps than anticipated."

Joshua now had exactly 27 days in which to prepare body and mind for the biggest fight of his career to date. There was a distinct sense of circularity about both the timing and venue for the Bakhtov showdown. It would be exactly a year and six days since he had made his bow in the paid ranks, and it was being staged at the O2 Arena, the scene of that maiden bout against Italy's Emanuele Leo and his destructive first-round triumph.

The whirlwind 12 months that followed had perhaps been even more successful than AJ or even his most ardent supporters could have hoped for, but as he contemplated his shot at the WBC International heavyweight belt, the man himself was studiously keeping his feet firmly on the ground.

"Not much [in life] has changed. I've got a lot more fans now, that's for sure, as I have boxed around the country, but I have been in the gym, so I haven't been able to see the impact. It's a basic lifestyle really.

"I am aware of the expectations around me and the potential that the great guys achieved. I'm at the start of my career like they all were and I

know that hard work is the key. If I keep my head down and work hard, I can reach the top. Training is 50 times harder than the fight.

"Bakhtov is a lot busier than my last opponent. I look at him the same as I looked at Matt Legg, one of my previous opponents, just with a lot more experience. Legg came out with a lot of hooks and gave it a go. Bakhtov can take punches for fun, and he'll be looking to get to me. Hopefully, he'll be the one eating a lot of shots."

Bakhtov's durability and willingness to come forward were borne out by his statistics. The 34-year-old from St Petersburg boasted a record of 38 wins in 47 fights, with 25 knockouts, and none of his nine defeats had come inside the first four rounds. Also, the Russian hadn't been stopped in the ring since 2005.

It seemed, then, that Bakhtov was the antithesis of the sacrificial lamb. Yet Joshua made a mockery of his opponent's solid record with a merciless performance that lasted a total of four minutes.

Neither man landed a meaningful blow in the first minute of the opening round, but that proved the calm before the storm. Joshua now unloaded a painful combination on his opponent in the corner. Bakhtov escaped the trap, but a few seconds later AJ unleashed a straight right that caught him square in the face and left him with an ominous-looking cut above his left eye. The Russian was so dazed by the blow that he temporarily stopped to shake his head with a mixture of disbelief and discomfort. The Olympic champion kept coming forward with intent, but Bakhtov made it to the bell and spent the interval in his corner, receiving frenzied attention to his widening cut.

The tone for the second round was set early. Bakhtov, perhaps sensing the inevitable, came out swinging – in the forlorn hope of turning the fight into a brawl and catching his rival with a lucky blow. Joshua accepted the invitation with obvious relish and proceeded to pulverize his opponent with punch after punch.

Less than a minute into the round, referee Ian John-Lewis briefly pulled the pair apart to check on Bakhtov's eye but allowed the fight to continue. AJ charged forward and again had his man cowering under another barrage of blows. This time there was no reprieve and John-Lewis stepped in to call a halt to proceedings.

Joshua was the new WBC International heavyweight champion. Just six years after first setting foot in a ring, the 24-year-old had his hands on a belt.

"The ruthless nature of Anthony Joshua the fighter was exposed for the first time after the demolition of veteran Denis Bakhtov at the O2 Arena in London, with the young heavyweight admitting his disappointment at not seeing the Russian 'on the floor, out cold'," wrote the *Daily Telegraph*'s Gareth A. Davies.

"Instead, the contest was stopped one minute into the second round with the 6ft 7in, 17st Olympic champion unloading on the wobbly Russian.

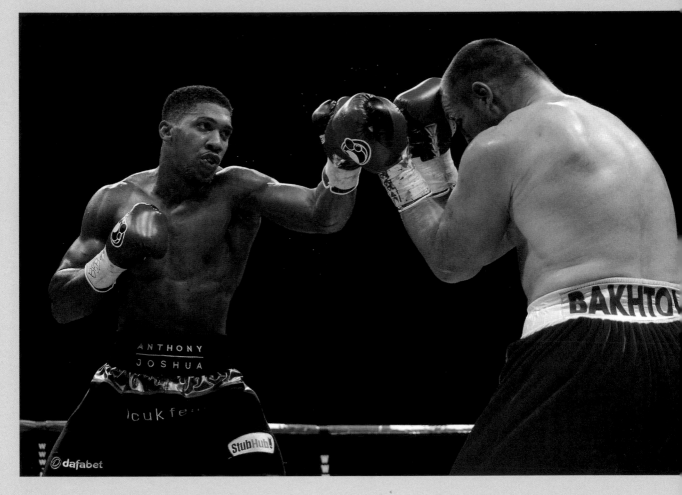

It was four minutes of brutality, through which Joshua grinned and stuck his tongue out.

"Still raw, Joshua was caught a couple of times on the inside, and by one left hook. But the work in progress continues to fascinate the boxing world's slumbering heavyweight division with his physique and power."

Joshua himself was more critical of his own performance. Despite his meteoric rise, he insisted that victory at the O2 was only a staging post in his boxing journey rather than a final destination.

"This, my first year, I've achieved nothing yet. I'm still the underdog. I just keep it simple, keep it hungry and crack on. What would I give myself out of 10 so far? A one. Why? It's only Year One. We've got years to go. Let me do that same thing to Klitschko, then I'd give myself a 10. That's Bakhtov, that's not Klitschko in there. He's not a world champion, is he?

"I took the odd punch and it's never smart to do that. Sometimes you can let the adrenaline get in the way and you want to see a bit of blood, whoever it's shedding from. I must stay calm and switched on."

ABOVE: Denis Bakhtov endured four minutes of pain at the hands of AJ in their WBC International heavyweight championship fight in October 2014.

FOLLOWING PAGES: Joshua claimed the first belt of his professional career after stopping Bakhtov after one minute of the second round at the O2.

" It only went two rounds, but I just wanted to hurt him. I don't like it when the referees step in and stop the fight. He hadn't been stopped, so I just wanted to see what he could take. He was a strong guy and he wasn't an easy opponent, but I wanted to make light work of him. I really enjoyed it. It's time to step it up, that's where the spitefulness is coming in. This is gladiator, the arena. There's a whole ocean of heavyweights out there. **"**

JOSHUA reacts to his victory over Denis Bakhtov to claim the vacant WBC International Heavyweight title

7 WORLD
CHAMPION

W**O**RLD CHAM**P**ION

Claiming the WBC international title was a significant achievement, but Joshua wanted much more. After six further triumphs following his win over Denis Bakhtov, it was confirmed that he would fight American Charles Martin for the coveted IBF heavyweight belt

There was precious little time, or probably inclination, for AJ to celebrate his victory over Denis Bakhtov at the O2 in October 2014. His next assignment against former British and Commonwealth champion Michael Sprott in Liverpool was the following month, and there was work to be done. It would be his 10th pro outing.

Sprott was just two months short of his 40th birthday when the two met. Despite never reaching the very upper echelons of the sport, he boasted a record of 42 wins in 64 bouts, in a career that had begun back in 1996. By contrast, Joshua had turned 25 the previous month and had exactly 35 minutes, 13 seconds of ring time under his belt. The gulf in experience was matched only by the chasm between the two in terms of power, and the way AJ dismantled his opponent was as brutal as it was mesmerizing.

The opening minute of the fight in the Echo Arena was misleadingly uneventful. Then, after allowing himself time to acclimatize, the newly crowned WBC International champion detonated and hammered Sprott backwards with a one-two combination to the head. The older man retreated desperately to the ropes, but there was nowhere to hide as Joshua surged forward with a salvo of punches to the face and body. After just 1 minute, 26 seconds, the referee intervened to spare the veteran any more punishment. It was Joshua's shortest bout so far.

He now boasted a perfect record – 10 out of 10 – and the only thing that seemed capable of derailing the Joshua juggernaut at this stage was his own body. His next scheduled fight was with the American Kevin "Kingpin" Johnson in January, but a stress fracture in his back put a temporary end to those plans. It was not until April 2015, five months after roughing up Sprott, that AJ returned to action.

His new opponent was also an American, Jason Gavern. The fight in the Metro Radio Arena in Newcastle proved to be a curate's egg: he put

his man down four times before the bout was stopped, but was taken into the third round for only the second time in his career.

Three of the quartet of knockdowns came in the second round, but it was the fourth that sealed the deal. It came courtesy of a thunderous left hook in the third stanza, which left the American unable to continue. The contest had lasted exactly 7 minutes and 21 seconds.

"I had a bit of ring rust so couldn't display everything I have been doing in the gym," the winner conceded. "But once the momentum gets going, I will be able to display some more shots, some more sharp shooting. There are a lot of expectations and Jason is a very awkward opponent. He's a slippery customer and he is there to make me look back and he did a good job of that. He was a defensive puzzle to unfold but I slowly broke him down."

Gavern headed home across the Atlantic for his next fight, leaving under no illusions about just how hard his opponent was capable of hitting.

"A lot of guys his size don't move as well as Joshua. He's 6 foot, 6 inches, 260 pounds and he's dancing around, throwing double jabs and triple left hooks. How is this guy doing this? For his size, he's very athletic. He grew two feet after the weigh-in, he was huge. In the middle of the ring I thought, 'Oh, my gosh'. I just tried to fight. He knocked me down three times but I kept getting up. The last punch I didn't remember until I saw it after the fight."

A month later, AJ was up against Brazilian Raphael Zumbano Love at the Barclaycard Arena in Birmingham. The rescheduled and higher-profile

LEFT: Joshua was dominant when he stepped into the ring against former British and Commonwealth champion Michael Sprott at Liverpool's Echo Arena in late 2014.

clash with Johnson was only 21 days away, though, so this fight was in truth more of a warm-up than meaningful challenge. The bout duly followed the script, Joshua spectacularly stopping his opponent just 1 minute, 21 seconds into the second round, with a fearsome straight right.

The end of the fight was not the end of the entertainment for the audience in Birmingham, however. Johnson climbed into the ring and the two men went face to face before the American threw down a very public gauntlet. "I've got the antidote for this guy," he announced. "I know what I've got to do to stop this guy. This will be the meanest fight anyone has seen."

The boxing world would discover in only three short weeks whether Johnson's bold claim would prove prophetic or foolhardy.

There was little doubt the 35-year-old American had the pedigree to back up his brash confidence. In his 36 professional outings before facing Joshua, he'd won 29 times and drawn once, and had never been stopped in his six losses. He'd fought Vitali Klitschko for the WBC heavyweight title in 2009 and taken the Ukrainian to 12 rounds, and he went the same distance in defeat to Tyson Fury in 2012.

The pre-fight verbal sparring undoubtedly generated an extra edge to the atmosphere inside the O2 Arena, the venue for the clash. The crowd had gleefully installed Johnson as Public Enemy Number 1 and the fans and media alike waited expectantly to see if the Kingpin could justify his bold prediction. "Can Kevin Johnson live up to all those words and take this fella deep?" asked Sky Sports commentator Nick Halling just before the bell. "It's scheduled for 10 rounds, but whether it goes that long remains to be seen."

The first round began cagily and then, after a minute, AJ rocked the American with a brutal right hook. The contest now became one-way traffic, the crowd favourite advancing and Johnson retreating warily. The tactic kept the American out of trouble until 20 seconds before the end of the round, when a close-range onslaught forced him down on one knee and he took the mandatory count. Joshua came again and with another savage assault floored his opponent at the same time as the bell sounded.

Johnson had to be helped back to his corner, and few who saw his slow, unsteady progress to his stool expected him to come out for the second. It was testament to his pride and bravery that he did, but the American barely threw a punch in the second stanza. AJ unloaded time and time again, and just 1 minute, 22 seconds into the round, the referee put him out of his misery.

Joshua's WBC International title was safe and he enjoyed a four-month break from the ring before his next bout. The venue for the September assignment was again the O2 Arena in London. His opponent was Scotland's Gary "Highlander" Cornish and both AJ's WBC crown and the vacant Commonwealth heavyweight belt were on the line.

The clash was notable because it was the first time Joshua had ever stepped into a ring with 12 scheduled rounds ahead of him. Any questions

about his potential stamina over such a distance were left unanswered, though: he required a mere 97 seconds to dispose of his opponent.

Cornish's record of 21 wins in 21, not to mention boasting both the height and weight to rival even AJ, meant that the neutral spectators had been hoping for a prolonged encounter. But a lightning right inside the first minute caught the Scot, shunting him down on his backside, and the writing was on the wall. He got to his feet – and was sent back down by another shuddering right. As he kneeled, staring at the canvas, there was no way back. He did get to his feet, but the referee refused to let the fight continue and Joshua had added the Commonwealth title to his collection in characteristically pyrotechnic style.

"There's no extra time," Joshua said after what was his 14th pro outing. "Credit to Gary where credit is due. He's a big man and had a solid jab. It's a 12-round fight and I wasn't trying to dish it all out in round one, but I managed to find shots to get the job done. I was trying to slip his long solid jabs and counter him and he went tumbling down. If I leave it and start taking my time, then it could be me on the end of those shots in five rounds' time."

AJ's final fight of 2015 was scheduled for December at the O2. Intriguingly, it saw him up against a familiar foe in the shape of Dillian Whyte, the man who had inflicted his first ever defeat on Joshua as an amateur in a pub in north London six years earlier. Whyte had turned professional in 2011, two years earlier than his old rival, and although his progress through the full-time ranks had not been spectacular, he went into the clash with an unbeaten record of 16 straight victories, 13 by knockout. If he could make it 17 and once again conquer Joshua, he would inherit his WBC and Commonwealth belts, as well as the British heavyweight title vacated by Tyson Fury.

The fight turned out to be a fascinating and at times acrimonious step into the unknown for AJ. The first round was AJ's thanks to a series of shuddering blows, and for the final minute of the opener it looked as though Whyte might not survive. The bad blood between the pair surfaced as the bell sounded when Joshua caught his old rival with a late shot. Whyte had to be held back by the referee as he tried to exact retribution, and both corners came piling into the ring in what was a brief but ugly mêlée.

Order was eventually restored. The second stanza then saw the aggressive Whyte twice catch his opponent with crunching shots that visibly hurt him. AJ was in a real fight now. The third round came and went, and for the first time in his career, Joshua was required to get up from his corner and fight in a fourth. It was time to fall back on all those countless hours of work in the gym.

Whyte continued to swing bravely and AJ was unable to put his man away. Not until midway through the seventh round did he finally deliver the coup de grâce. A big right rocked Whyte and Joshua sensed his moment, piling forward with a flurry of punches and then delivering a thunderous

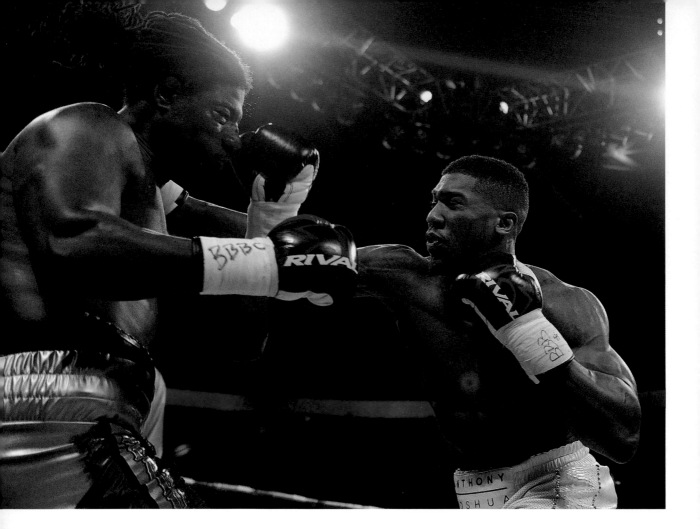

right uppercut that left his rival prostrate on the canvas. It was all over: AJ had his 15th pro win, the British heavyweight title and revenge for that loss to Whyte six years earlier.

"Dillian was a perfect fight for this stage. I'm going to keep on building and building until I make my mark in this heavyweight division. I found my way, found my rhythm. I had the same power that I had in the first round in the seventh. I learned stuff about myself and I can take that into 2016.

"Becoming an elite athlete in such a tough sport, it doesn't happen overnight, but I've got the desire, ambition and the team around me to do it. But I don't want to rush it because when I get there, I want to stay there. A world title fight is still far away."

It was not, however, quite as far off as he believed. In February 2016, just two months after his dust-up with Whyte, Matchroom announced that their man would face the unbeaten American Charles Martin for his IBF heavyweight title at the O2 in April. Joshua's big chance had arrived.

"Fighting for the heavyweight world title has been a dream of mine since I turned professional. I feel privileged to have the opportunity to turn that dream into reality. Martin is a great fighter and a hungry competitor, so I am going to have to produce the performance of my career to claim that belt."

The first southpaw Joshua had faced in his career, Martin had a record that was certainly impressive: 23 wins and a draw. He had claimed the vacant IBF belt after stopping Ukrainian Vyacheslav Glazkov in January in New York City. The fight at the O2 would be his first bout outside the States, and the 29-year-old was in buoyant mood ahead of the first defence of his world title.

"I'm going to say I know I can touch his. I know I can test it, I know I can knock him out. That's the confidence that I walk this earth with. This is my profession, this is my livelihood, this is how I feed my kids. When I step into the ring, I'm going to go to work and do what I do best. He's going to feel my presence right away."

Martin entered the ring wearing a tall crown, a fur-trimmed, velvet cape and a big smile. It was a brash entrance, but once the champion disrobed, it was time for the serious business.

The opening round was a tentative affair. Both men probed cautiously, neither unleashing anything significant. After three inconclusive minutes, they headed to their corners, and no one inside the O2 was any wiser about how the fight might unfold. The second stanza would be the polar opposite.

Joshua looked more purposeful from the start. With a minute on the clock, he caught Martin full in the face with a lightning right hand that the American never saw coming and which sent him tumbling to the floor. The champion took the count on one knee and returned to the fray, but just 15 seconds later was caught with a replay of the first punch. Once again, he hit the deck. This time Martin did not beat the count. After just 1 minute, 32 seconds of the second round, AJ was officially a world champion.

"I mean business and I'm here to stay," Joshua said after his convincing victory. "There's still a lot of work to be done. I've done two rounds, so I'll go to the changing rooms and work on the pads. I've got people like David Haye and Tyson Fury calling me out, so I need to keep improving. Every fight gets better and better. I want to give value for money and I appreciate the ongoing support of the fans."

Defeat for Martin brought to an end his brief, three-month reign as IBF heavyweight champion and he conceded that AJ was a worthy winner. "He was the better man tonight. I got hit with a right hand I didn't see and that cost the fight. He's a great fighter, but it was just that his right hand was fast. I didn't see the shot. He had good speed."

AJ's spectacular success was history in the making. In knocking down Martin, he became only the fourth heavyweight ever to win a world title while still a reigning Olympic champion, joining an exclusive club that had previously featured only the legends Floyd Patterson, Muhammad Ali and Leon Spinks. He also became the first British boxer to complete the fabled double.

The 26-year-old from Watford was British boxing's golden boy. Ambitious plans to unify the division and elevate himself to undisputed heavyweight champion status were now gathering pace. The last British man to have done so was Lennox Lewis in 1999, and AJ was now on a mission to emulate his friend and mentor.

FOLLOWING PAGES: AJ is all smiles as he shows off the IBF World Championship belt after taking a little more than 4½ minutes to knock out Charles Martin at the O2 Arena in London in April 2016; it took him less than four years to go from Olympic gold medallist to a world champion at boxing's most glamorous weight.

" Anthony Joshua launched himself into British superstardom and world-title glory with two booming right hooks in the second round to send 20,000 fans into rapture here last night and leave the hapless defending champion Charles Martin flattened. It is 30 years since Mike Tyson savaged Trevor Berbick inside two rounds to become the youngest heavyweight champion in history, and Joshua's mauling of Martin had the same brutal undertones. The young Londoner has an altogether different muscularity and feel, but his presence and poise is being articulated with powerful brutality. **"**

GARETH A DAVIES writing in the Daily Telegraph *after AJ is crowned IBF world heavyweight champion*

8 EPIC KLITSCHKO BATTLE

AJ's IBF triumph had propelled him into the top of echelons of the sport, but he now had to fight one of the division's biggest beasts to prove himself a truly great heavyweight

It had taken Joshua just 16 fights and less than three years to transform himself from inexperienced professional debutant into a world champion. It was by any measure a remarkable and rapid career arc, but AJ viewed his victory over Charles Martin as the beginning of a new chapter rather than the culmination of his efforts. The 26-year-old wanted more belts.

By taking the IBF title in April 2016, he became one of three world champions at the time. The American Deontay Wilder was in possession of the WBC belt while fellow Brit Tyson Fury was the holder of the WBO, IBO and WBA versions. Both men were firmly in his sights, but the politics of boxing is nothing if not complex and he first had to defend his own title.

The man selected as the first challenger was an American named Dominic Breazeale, and the pair were scheduled to fight at the O2 in June. With an unbeaten record in his 17 professional bouts and standing at six foot seven, Breazeale seemed a daunting prospect. However, he had beaten no one of real note and many confidently predicted a comfortable evening's work for AJ in east London.

The champion did successfully defend his crown, though the clash did not quite follow the script.

The opening two rounds saw Joshua work his jab effectively, and a couple of left hooks certainly rocked the challenger from across the Atlantic. By the end of the fourth, Breazeale was sporting a swollen eye, but he was still standing. He even caught Joshua with a decent right in the fifth. Not until the seventh round was the champion finally able to make his superior power tell, catching the challenger with an explosive left that reduced him to a crumpled heap on the canvas.

RIGHT: American Dominic Breazeale proved a stern test for Joshua in London in June 2016 before the champion finally stopped his man in the seventh round.

It was only the second time AJ had been taken so deep into a fight, his seven-round clash with Dillian Whyte in December having lasted 26 seconds longer. He admitted afterwards that he was feeling the effects of his hectic schedule, which had seen him box five times in the space of 13 months.

"It's been tough. I only had two weeks off after my last fight and got straight back in the gym. I can have a nice little break for once and come back with recharged batteries. I'm tired, but now I can get some rest and recharge my batteries and start afresh again."

Joshua headed off for a well-earned holiday – while his promoter Eddie Hearn remained hard at work, trying to line up the next opponent. Boxing's politics did not make this a straightforward job. Hearn was reluctant to put AJ in with the big-hitting Deontay Wilder at this stage of his career, and events elsewhere only complicated the picture.

In September 2016, Fury pulled out of his scheduled rematch with Wladimir Klitschko for a second time after being declared medically unfit to fight and testing positive for cocaine. The following month, the Mancunian relinquished the three belts he'd taken from Klitschko in 2015. Talks now began between Matchroom and the Ukrainian for a potential showdown for AJ's IBF title, as well as the now vacant WBA and IBO crowns.

The problem was that the bout required sanctioning by the WBA as a unification contest and their blessing was not initially forthcoming. Negotiations finally broke the deadlock and a clash was preliminarily pencilled in for December 2016. Klitschko then injured his calf in training, and Hearn scrambled frantically for a new opponent.

The man to step forward to fight at the Manchester Arena in December was the 34-year-old Éric Molina. The Texan had won 25 of his 28 fights, 19 by knockout, so he seemed a worthy opponent. Ultimately, he would provide little more than a footnote in the AJ story, lasting less than three rounds when the pair came face to face in the north-west 15 days before Christmas.

Klitschko was ringside to watch the fight and witnessed his one-time sparring partner at his imperious best. The first two stanzas saw AJ land plenty of blows, but it was in the third that he really got through Molina's defences. A right-left combination opened up the American before he was obliterated by a straight right. He recovered sufficiently to continue, but was subjected to a trademark barrage of left and rights from the champion and turned his back on Joshua. The referee took his signal and stopped the bout.

After AJ's 18th professional victory, Hearn invited Klitschko into the ring and announced that the fight between the two men would take place at Wembley Stadium in April 2017. "It's been an arduous wait to gain official approval," Hearn said, "but we were delighted to receive the news that the WBA will officially sanction the fight between Anthony Joshua and Wladimir Klitschko for the WBA super title."

The fight that everyone wanted to see was finally on! The two men now had four months in which to prepare for what promised to be a titanic showdown.

The magnitude of the challenge Klitschko represented was staggering. The Ukrainian was the undisputed standout heavyweight of his generation. Though his points decision defeat to Fury in Dusseldorf in 2015 meant that he was coming into the fight without a belt to his name, he had previously held at least one version of the division's world title for 15 straight years. He had been the IBF champion for nine uninterrupted years, seven months and six days, making 18 successful defences of his crown. Only the late, great American Joe Louis had retained a world heavyweight title for longer.

Like AJ, he was a former Olympic super-heavyweight champion (after victory in Atlanta in 1996), and he had contested a grand total of 28 world title fights. Prior to that, his 68 professional bouts had brought the Ukrainian 64 victories, 53 of them by knockout. The pair may have sparred before, but Klitschko was nothing like anyone Joshua had faced competitively.

The build-up to the clash was notable for the lack of animosity, staged or otherwise, between the two protagonists. There was a steely

BELOW: AJ
intensified his
training regime
ahead of his pivotal
clash with Wladimir
Klitschko at
Wembley Stadium,
the 19th fight of his
professional career.

determination from both men, but the pre-fight press conferences were more articulate and, as a result, more revealing than boxing fans expected.

"Boxing is a violent sport but we all can be friendly with each other," Klitschko told the media. "Respect is never going to get lost, but once that bell rings, one man needs to go down and the other needs to conquer. When the last bell rings, we will shake hands again. In between, on the night, we will be enemies. We will definitely show the world that despite the violence, we can handle each other respectfully before and after.

"This is a big step for AJ. He hasn't fought this type of quality fighter yet. It's going to be challenging for him, and it's going to be challenging for me. This fight is fifty-fifty, both fighters have a chance to win the fight, but I have this feeling that this is my night.

"I'm the challenger again. I feel young, hungry, humble and totally obsessed with my goal to raise my hands again. I'm so obsessed with winning. I realized that life is a circle, and I see myself in AJ. I do believe I know how he thinks, how he goes, and how the actual fight is going to be.

"The belts are very important. I've been attached to these belts for a very long time. The only difference is in my last fight they went to the opposite corner. So my goal and obsession is for those belts to land in my corner, in my hands. Obsession is love in extreme shape. I'm in love with my goal."

For AJ, the build-up was characterized by questions about how he would cope with the gulf in top-level experience between himself and his decorated opponent. After all, he was 14 years Klitschko's junior. What's more, with 49 fewer professional fights under his belt, he had much less ring guile.

"Let's strip it right back to what it is – a young lion, ferocious, hungry, very determined," he said. "I left no stone unturned in training camp.

Someone is going to win and someone is going to continue with their career and I'm very confident that's me.

"Even though it's an amazing event I try to strip everything back down. It's me and a man coming to blows – and the best man will win. I'm preparing physically and mentally for any battle. That's why I enjoy the sport and take it seriously. It is just another stepping stone towards greatness. I'm only going to be myself – the fight is already as big as it can be.

"There are belts on the line, there's legacy on the line, there's 12 rounds of intense, ferocious boxing on the line. It comes with everything you want to see – boxing skills, power, timing. It's just how long you can last and withstand each other's abilities."

There was nothing to choose between the two in terms of height, both men six foot six. Joshua just had the edge on the scales, weighing in at 250 pounds for the big fight against the 41-year-old Klitschko at 240.5 pounds. Neither, then, had a clear physical advantage. It would, most agreed, be a contest decided by the relative merits of AJ's youthful dynamism against the Ukrainian's battle-hardened experience.

A post-war British record of 90,000 people crammed into Wembley on 29 April 2017 for the clash. Millions more would watch in the 150 countries worldwide who televised the £30 million bout. The time had come to discover whether Joshua was the real deal.

He emerged from the famous Wembley tunnel wearing a white robe over white shorts, boots and gloves. Before entering the ring, he was hoisted aloft on a hydraulic platform to greet the cheering, partisan crowd, flanked either side by the flaming letters "A" and "J". The home of football was ready for the biggest night ever in British boxing history. Smiling and

" You can't deny it, this is epic. As much as I'm calm, when I look around and see how pumped people are for this fight, it gives me energy, it gives me life. "

JOSHUA looks ahead to the Klitschko fight

waving to his legion of supporters, the favourite was a picture of calm, despite an expectant atmosphere that could have crushed him.

The start of the first round was greeted by a collective roar inside Wembley. Both boxers tried to establish an early dominance with their respective left-hand jabs, but in those eagerly anticipated first three minutes neither man was prepared to overcommit to the attack. In the second stanza, Klitschko caught Joshua with a right, who recovered to edge the round. He then emerged for the third round in more aggressive mood and put the Ukrainian on the back foot with a series of accurate one-two combinations. The fourth saw a subtle shift in momentum: Klitschko threw more punches and shook his opponent with a crunching straight right.

The match was still incredibly tight, though, and the tension that had built dramatically exploded in the fifth. It began at a frenetic pace as AJ launched a barrage of powerful blows, forcing the Ukrainian to retreat. There was nowhere to hide and after only 29 seconds Klitschko crumpled to the floor under the weight of the onslaught. He took the count but he was now sporting a cut around his left eye. Incredibly he got up and, rather than duck for cover, mounted a counter-attack, landing a vicious left hook that visibly stunned Joshua. Suddenly, the veteran was in the ascendency. A straight right from the Ukrainian underlined the shift in power, and for the remainder of the round the question was whether AJ had the stamina and courage to survive. He made it to the bell, but it was a close-run thing.

Boxing expert Steve Bunce was ringside for the fight and had a privileged point of view of the fifth round. "Klitschko marks up, his legs start to go and finally, after a 30-second assault, he collapses in front of me," he wrote on the BBC Sport website. "I swear I have some of his blood on my notepad. He has a cut, he's pawing at one of the ropes to get up. There is one second, with everyone on their feet, I had a moment of genius and looked across at Joshua. He was draped in the other corner like he was unconscious and exhausted. Joshua was finished. At the end of that round, having dropped Klitschko, that's the round where Joshua's trainer said he was most scared as his man was utterly exhausted."

The sixth round was another traumatic one for AJ and his corner. For the first minute, both men were seemingly still drawing breath from their previous exertions. Then, after 70 seconds, Klitschko suddenly detonated a booming right hand that shredded Joshua's defences and dumped him unceremoniously on the canvas. For the first time in 19 professional fights, the champion had been put down. As he stared at the floor on his hands and knees, it looked like the fairytale could be over. He struggled to his feet but Klitschko sensed his chance and stormed forward for the rest of the round. For the remaining minute-and-a-half, AJ clung on – and made it to the bell.

"I maintain that when Joshua gets knocked down in that sixth round, he is out cold," Bunce wrote. "He goes down, wakes up as he hits the floor and then survives the round as both of them are wrecked. They fight on, struggle on."

The seventh stanza saw Joshua again on the back foot. He was clearly still feeling the effects of the knockdown and he lacked his trademark speed and accuracy. The eighth round was the deepest AJ had ever been taken since joining the professional ranks and he was hurt again by another Klitschko right hand. By the ninth, though, he seemed to have recovered, rediscovering his range with the jab to regain some momentum. The 10th round was his as he slowed the Ukrainian with a series of body shots. Now, with potentially only six minutes of action left, the outcome was still uncertain.

The penultimate stanza began in similar style to the fifth, Joshua tearing out of his corner and unleashing on his opponent. Klitschko was in full retreat, and 70 seconds into the round AJ launched a devastating uppercut from close range. The champion followed up with further painful blows, and for the second time in the evening, his opponent was on the floor. Somehow Klitschko, a great former champion, found the strength and courage to get up, but his opponent produced a muscular right uppercut followed by a horizontal left hook and the Ukrainian was on the canvas for a third time. Again he refused to quit, but he was soon trapped in the corner under a sustained salvo of savage punches from his opponent. With 23 seconds left on the clock, referee David Fields stepped in to end the fight. At the time of the stoppage, Joshua was up 96-93 and 95-93 on two cards, with Klitschko leading 95-93 on the other.

Anthony Joshua was the new, unified WBA, IBF and IBO world champion – and a new era for heavyweight boxing had begun.

"I knew it was possible to hurt him, but I am learning round by round," he said. "I'm learning under the bright lights. I don't come to box, I come to hurt people. With all due respect, I came to hurt him. At the end of the day, I figured out what I had to do and got him done.

"There's been many a time in training when we go into the 11th round and I'm tired but I know I have to keep it up because I have to go the distance. I showed tonight that fights are won in the gym. It gets tough and boxing isn't easy. You have to have the whole package. I don't mind fighting him again, if he wants the rematch. Big respect to Wladimir for challenging the young lions of the division."

Defeat for Klitschko ended his dream of regaining the belts he'd lost to Fury in 2015. Philosophical about the result, he conceded in his post-fight interview that he had spurned his best chance of victory after knocking down AJ in the sixth round.

"I thought he wouldn't get up," he confessed. "I think I should have done more straight after he went down. But I was pretty sure it was going to be my night, so I took my time. I think Joshua and I both did great. I think we did a lot for the sport in the way we performed and how we respected and treated each other. It was a great night for boxing and the fans.

"Tonight, we all won. I didn't get the belts, but I didn't feel like I lost – not my name, my face, nor my reputation. It was great to be involved in such an amazing occasion. I have always been a fan of AJ's talent. He beat me and he won the fight, shows his qualities. The best man won and it's a massive event for boxing. Two gentlemen fought each other. Anthony was better. It's really sad I didn't make it. He is unified champion and I have to cheer up. He did what he was supposed to do."

Victory instantly catapulted AJ into the realms of global superstar. The reaction in the media in the wake of the fight was as emphatic as his destructive display in the final round at Wembley.

"From the moment the final blows of a magnificent fight rippled down Anthony Joshua's 27-year-old arms on to the bleeding and battered head of the 41-year-old Wladimir Klitschko in the 11th round, there could be no more arguments about who is the best heavyweight in the world," wrote Kevin Mitchell in *The Guardian*.

"It was not just that Joshua, unbeaten in all 19 professional fights, had added the WBA super version of the title to his own IBF belt, or even that he had stopped one of boxing's finest old champions. What secured the winner's acclaim was that he got up from a right cross in the sixth that would have felled an elephant.

"Probably unsure what city he was in, he fought on through a daze to bring the contest to the most dramatic conclusion, and will rule until someone of equal stature unseats him. There is nobody of that calibre on the horizon."

“ I'm not perfect, but I'm trying and, if you don't take part, you're going to fail. Boxing is about character. There is nowhere to hide. No complications about boxing. Anyone can do this. Give it a go. You leave your ego at the door. Massive respect to Klitschko. He's a role model in and out of the ring and I've got nothing but love and respect for anyone who steps in the ring. London, I love you. Can I go home now? **”**

AJ talks to the Wembley crowd after his dramatic victory over Wladimir Klitschko

William HILL
matchroomboxing
sky sports box office
JDSPORTS.COM
ANTHONY
ANTHONY JOSHUA
LEONE
RIVAL
StubHub

9 DEFENDING
HIS CROWN

Champions are there to be challenged. AJ, the new holder of the WBA, IBF and IBO belts, knew that it would not be long before he would have to step back into the ring and put his three world titles on the line

As Joshua stood victorious inside the ring at Wembley Stadium in April 2017, basking in the glow of his career-defining defeat of Klitschko, there was a certain name not far from his and everyone else's lips. "Tyson Fury," he shouted out to the 90,000-strong crowd gathered at the home of football, "where you at, baby? Come on."

It may have been six months since Fury had relinquished the WBA, WBO, IBO titles – claimed after his own victory over Klitschko in late 2015 – but his shadow, all six foot nine of it, still loomed large over the heavyweight division. Fight fans were now licking their lips at the prospect of what would be the biggest bout in the history of British boxing.

The reality, however, was that Fury could not challenge AJ. Pending an investigation into doping and medical issues, his licence had been suspended the previous October by the British Boxing Board of Control. Eddie Hearn and Matchroom would have to look elsewhere for the first fighter to face the newly crowned champion.

In the months that followed, there was intense speculation about who the challenger would be. A rematch with Klitschko was potentially on the cards and would have been a popular choice, but in August the veteran Ukrainian confirmed that his glittering 21-year professional career was officially over. Hearn had to return to the drawing board. The following month, he announced that AJ would fight Bulgarian Kubrat Pulev in Cardiff at the end of October.

The 36-year-old from Sofia promised to be a genuine threat to Joshua's unbeaten record. He was the two-time European heavyweight champion, having claimed the title for a second time in 2016 after outpointing Dereck Chisora in Hamburg. Now the IBF's No. 1 challenger, he had been beaten only once in a 26-fight career. It spoke volumes about his pedigree

> **“** He's a star in his own country, he's like a king in Bulgaria. He's an Olympic bronze medallist which shows his pedigree. He's very, very talented. **”**

AJ ahead of his title defence against Kubrat Pulev in Cardiff

that the solitary loss, in 2014, came in a world title bout against the great Klitschko himself.

"It can't come soon enough," Joshua said after the announcement. "I have been eager to get back in the ring since Wembley and now we are confirmed and ready. I'll be locked away, focusing on fight Number 20 for the next eight weeks. I am excited to experience the atmosphere in a sold-out Principality Stadium and aim to give the fans a spectacular night."

His opponent, nicknamed "The Cobra", was in buoyant mood after the confirmation that he now had a second shot at a world belt. He predicted a confrontational fight – and one that he would win. "Anthony is a formidable opponent. We will not hug and hold, we will not run. We will stand and fight. His style fits mine perfectly, and in boxing, styles make fights. My preparation will be very intense, and I will be perfectly ready when I enter the ring so that he will have no chance to beat me."

Both men duly retreated to put in the hard work in the gym. Then, just 12 days before they were scheduled to meet in the Principality, it was revealed that Pulev had injured his shoulder in sparring. At the 11th hour, Cameroonian-French heavyweight Carlos Takam was drafted in as a replacement.

"I received a call from [Pulev's promoter] Kalle Sauerland to inform me that Pulev had injured his shoulder and may be ruled out of the fight – this was later confirmed by his doctor," explained Hearn. "IBF rules state that the mandatory will go to the next fighter in line, which is Carlos Takam.

"When the Pulev fight was announced I made a deal with Takam's team to begin camp and be on standby for this fight. When I called them they were overjoyed and good to go. It's a difficult position for AJ. Having prepared meticulously for the style and height of Pulev, he now faces a completely different style and challenge in Takam. This hasn't happened in his career before, but he is ready for all comers."

The physical contrast between Pulev and Takam was undeniably stark. Two-and-a-half inches shorter than the injured Bulgarian, the new challenger was an altogether stockier and more muscular opponent for the champion. Although he had not previously boxed for a world title, he had represented Cameroon at the 2004 Olympics, and in 35 pro fights, he had been beaten only three times. One of those three defeats came in May 2016, when he took New Zealand's Joseph Parker 12 rounds in Auckland. It was testament to his pedigree that just seven months later Parker was crowned WBO world champion.

The late change in fighters was far from ideal for Joshua, who had celebrated his 28th birthday earlier in the month. Now facing a very different tactical and physical challenge in the form of Takam, he had precious little time to adjust his training regime in the build-up to the first defence of his three titles. It was not a change that seemed to unduly unsettle the defending champion.

"Believe it or not, I still have the mindset of a challenger. I don't walk around with an ego just because I have a few belts on my shoulder. I know he has that mindset to find a way to win. If you keep on knocking on the door, you find a way through. I just have to boot him out because he isn't coming through this door.

"I'm still developing. I think that's why people jump at the opportunity. If I trash-talked more, I may be more feared. But my job is to break them

down in the ring, strip them of confidence, strip them of desire and strip them of winning.

"We're going to have a war. We're going to wear our hearts on our sleeves. This is what fighting's about. With me, it ain't about all this other stuff that goes on outside the ring. When people come to watch me box, they know they're going to have a good time. They know they're going to see knockouts."

Joshua weighed in at 18 stone 2 pounds for the fight, the heaviest he'd ever been. The challenger tipped the scales at a more modest 16 stone 11 pounds. Takam was conceding a significant weight and height advantage. Despite the slightly chaotic nature of his belated call-up, he insisted he was not filling the void left by Pulev simply for the money.

"I've been waiting for this opportunity for a long time. I'm ready for this fight. I'm ready for everything he has. We were in the gym getting ready, hoping we would get this chance. He's a world champion, he's earned his belt, but I'm coming here to take it. You have to defend your title and I'm not going to make it easy. I'm going to make this the fight of the year.

"If I can do things differently from what other boxers have done against him, I'll have a chance to win by knockout. A lot of people have asked me if I see any weaknesses in Joshua's style. All I can say is we will see on fight night. I'm not bothered about fighting in front of 80,000 people. The only people in the ring will be myself and Joshua. Nothing else matters except us."

His estimate of the assembled audience under the closed roof of the Principality Stadium was slightly generous, but the 78,000 fight fans in Cardiff in October was nonetheless a world record for an indoor boxing crowd, eclipsing the 63,315 spectators who had descended on the New Orleans Superdome back in 1978 to witness Muhammad Ali beat Leon Spinks.

The roar of the 78,000 was amplified by the enclosed nature of the venue as AJ made his way to the ring. Although his walk-on music failed to play, the fight began in otherwise familiar fashion, the champion working his jab effectively in the opening round. Takam concentrated on avoiding trouble, and Joshua took the round on the scorecard despite an absence of any real hostilities.

The second stanza was altogether more eventful: Takam came out with more aggression and ambition and broke the champion's nose. This was not the result of his glove work, though. Rather, it was the result of a flailing left hook to his body, which unbalanced him and propelled him headfirst into AJ's face. Most watching agreed the collision was clumsy but ultimately accidental, but Takam had left his mark: blood streamed from AJ's nose. Referee Phil Edwards issued a rebuke.

Patched up and good to go, Joshua returned to the jab in the third. Then, in the fourth round, he turned on the power to stamp his authority on proceedings. A potentially destructive right hook was partially blocked by Takam, then AJ pressed forward and unleashed an uppercut followed by a booming left hook, which left his man prone on the canvas. The Cameroonian-born Frenchman beat the count, returning to his corner at the end of the round with a serious cut above his right eye.

As the bell sounded for the start of the fifth stanza, the crowd sensed the end was imminent. A lack of accuracy from the champion, coupled with Takam's obdurateness, saw him survive the three minutes and although his cut required frenzied attention during the break, he came out for the next round.

Joshua was now the dominant force in the fight and he inflicted more visible damage on his opponent in the sixth, opening up a new cut around his right eye. Still Takam refused to buckle under the sustained pressure, and by the end of the eighth, those witnessing events were left in awe of the challenger's sheer courage and single-mindedness.

"Left and rights into Takam's body follow and Takam, with a battered left eye, with a battered right eye, waves his opponent on," reported the BBC Sport website at the end of the eighth round. "He wants more. Insane bravery and guts from the challenger. Warrior status.

"The doctors have another look at the substantial damage done to Takam's face. He deserves to be allowed to carry on, if he wants to, and he is allowed to. On we go."

A left hook/straight right combination in the proved there was some offensive life yet in Takam, but AJ remained largely on the front foot even

sky sports box office
matchroomboxing
William HILL
ANTHONY
JOSHUA
RIVAL
sky sports box office
William HILL
sky sports box office
matchroomboxing

ANTHONY
ANTHONY
William Hill
William Hill
LEONE
TAKAM
ANTHONY
JOSHUA
matchroomboxing
William Hill
sky sports
box office
ANTHONY
sky sports

though he was still unable to put his man away. For only the second time in his career, Joshua was heading into a 10th round.

Takam's heroic resistance undoubtedly endeared him to the Cardiff crowd, but his fairytale finally came to an end midway through the tenth. Two big lefts from the champion piled on the pressure and as AJ surged forward, the battered and bruised challenger could no longer summon the energy to fire anything back at him. The referee came between the two fighters. Joshua had successfully defended his WBA, IBF and IBO world heavyweight titles – but he had been made to work harder than anticipated.

The decision to stop the contest was greeted by jeers in certain sections of the crowd. Their displeasure, though, was aimed at neither the champion nor Takam. The fans were simply upset not to see such an epic encounter go the full distance. Given the damage the challenger had sustained, it was probably the right decision.

Takam begged to differ. "I don't know why the referee stopped the match. I respect the champion and the UK fans, they are great fans and I am happy to box here, but I don't know why they stopped it. I want a rematch. I make my preparations with 12 days to fight Anthony and I want to box him again."

Joshua admitted he was ultimately a relieved man to get his first multiple title defence out of the way. He refused to become embroiled in the debate over the referee's decision and insisted his main concern was getting the fight finished despite struggling with his broken nose.

"I come to fight. I don't sit on the edge and make decisions. It was a good fight until the ref stopped it, so I have the utmost respect for Takam. I have no interest in what's going on with the officials. That's not my job. My job is to worry about my opponent. I was watching him. I was trying to take him down round by round and unfortunately the ref stopped it before.

"I couldn't breathe [because of his nose]. He started catching up in the later rounds and it would've been a massive disaster, so I had to keep my cool. I have a couple of months to heel it up. I'm going to see some good doctors to crack it back into place."

Reaction to AJ's triumph was not quite as euphoric as it had been six months earlier when he defeated Klitschko. Even so, there was widespread agreement that his win was just the beginning of a long reign as the unified, and potentially in the future undisputed, world heavyweight champion.

"Joshua had thrown everything at the super-sub with the tank-like physique and granite chin, but he was beginning to tire when Edwards stepped in to bring the fight to a close, much to Takam's fury," wrote Gareth A. Davies in the *Daily Telegraph*. "At the end of it all the young man who is fast becoming a superstar now has a record which reads 20 fights, 20 stoppages.

"But Takam proved a tough man to put down, with Joshua only able to put him away in the 10th when Edwards felt Takam had taken enough punishment after a right nearly knocked him off his feet. It seemed premature, but Joshua's bandwagon goes marching on."

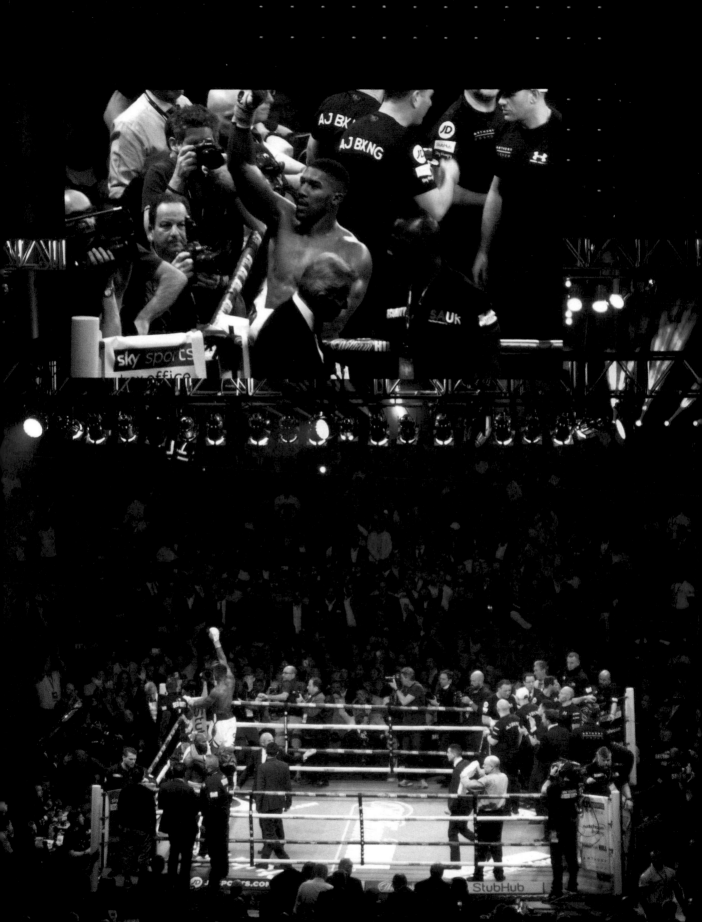

" This was just the type of fight, experience and adversity that Anthony Joshua needed. He wasn't at his best, but you won't always be and it's those times you have to find a way. Some fall apart after a broken nose, but he remained composed and controlled the fight. It would have been nice just to let it play out one way or another because Takam still looked strong. It was a very good test for AJ, though, especially with the broken nose. **"**

LENNOX LEWIS, former undisputed world heavyweight champion, on Joshua's victory over Carlos Takam

ABOVE: Anthony Joshua's eagerly anticipated title defence against the unbeaten New Zealander Joseph Parker in Cardiff was his third fight in the Principality since he turned professional.

Joshua's work for 2017 was done, but in January the next chapter in his career became clearer when it was announced his 21st and most seminal fight yet would be against New Zealand's unbeaten Joseph Parker at the end of March. AJ would return to Cardiff and the Principality Stadium for the bout and this time it was not only Joshua's titles that would be on the line.

Victorious in all 24 of his pro fights, Parker had claimed the WBO heavyweight belt by beating American Andy Ruiz in Auckland in December 2016. He had twice successfully defended his crown before the confirmation he would cross swords with AJ, and that meant their

Principality showdown would be a unification fight for three of the division's four biggest belts. It would be the first time in history two reigning heavyweight champions had met in Britain and also the first time since 1987, when Mike Tyson outpointed Tony Tucker in Las Vegas, that two unbeaten heavyweight champions had stepped into the ring together.

The build-up to the clash saw AJ installed as the firm favourite to extend his unbeaten record, but with Parker boasting 18 knockouts in his 24 fights, Joshua was under no illusions; his Kiwi opponent represented a genuine threat to his status as the division's top dog.

ABOVE: The WBO world champion Joseph Parker stepped into the ring to face Anthony Joshua in Cardiff's Principality Stadium in March 2018 boasting a record of 24 wins in 24 fights.

"People should never overlook Joseph Parker," he said. "He's a world champion, undefeated, and he has that Kiwi blood. That's a triple threat. I'm taking this deadly serious, and I'm focused on the task ahead.

"Anyone I fight, they always come 30 per cent better than what I've seen so I can't expect the same old Parker in the ring. That's where my goal is and that's where I'm focused on. I can't take my eye off this guy. He's talented and he wants to prove himself."

Joshua weighed in at 17 stone and four pounds for the fight, almost a stone lighter than he had been for his clash with Takam, but he was still heavier than his Kiwi opponent and with a significant height and reach advantage, the champion looked supremely prepared for the challenge ahead.

A boisterous crowd of 78,000 inside the Principality Stadium were on their feet when AJ emerged from the dressing room, and the fight that unfolded in front of them was as engrossing as it was tactical as the two men in the ring both showed their quality, resolve and durability.

AJ's left jab ensured Parker was rarely allowed inside his defences to unload from close range, but the challenger was unperturbed as he repeatedly came forward looking for an opening. Joshua's respect for his opponent was obvious and although he was ahead on the scorecards from the opening round, the home favourite resisted the temptation to gamble everything on a decisive assault.

Two big left hooks from the champion in the 10th gave the crowd reason to cheer, only for Parker to connect with a good shot of his own in the eleventh, but there was to be no early conclusion to proceedings and for the first time in his career, AJ was taken the full 12 rounds.

The judges would decide the winner but there was no real doubt Joshua was the victor and the scorecards, reading 118-110, 118-110 and 119-109 in his favour, confirmed his superiority on the night. AJ was now the unified WBA, IBF and WBO world heavyweight champion.

"There's a lot more to come," he said after his twenty-first straight win since turning professional. "We have to roll with the punches. I am developing. My amateur career was three-and-a-half years. This October is five years as a pro. In boxing I have always put my heart on my sleeve and showed the world good and bad. I will always be honest, give you who I am and my best. Everyone will enjoy this journey and you'll see the good, bad and ugly. If I can keep controlling fighters like that, I will be about a long time."

It was not in truth the most pyrotechnic performance of his career, but it did reflect the champion's growing maturity. "I thought it was an assured performance from Joshua," wrote the BBC's boxing correspondent Mike Costello. "He clearly thought early on that he may be going the distance and adjusted his pace to suit. We also have to consider that Parker for long periods, as game and as resilient as he was, appeared to be in damage limitation mode."

" I knew how to break him down and put him in a position so he couldn't give much back. Every time he came forward I just rammed that jab in his face. We've always been in at the deep end with high expectations. I just focus on improving. I know the expectations of what I can achieve are very possible but without dedication they won't happen. The sky is the limit. I'm not elated because I don't let the highs get to my head. We have to go again soon. **"**

AJ looks ahead after victory over Joseph Parker in Cardiff

10 | WHAT NEXT
FOR AJ?

WHAT NEXT FOR AJ?

The future is bright for Britain's triple heavyweight world champion both in and out of the ring as he strives to cement his reputation as one of boxing's greatest ever fighters

Victory over Joseph Parker in Cardiff underlined AJ's status as the best heavyweight on the planet, but the WBC belt held by American Deontay Wilder still eluded him.

In the three-decade-long era of heavyweight boxing's quartet of major titles – the WBA, IBF, WBO and WBC – no fighter has ever laid claim to all four belts simultaneously. AJ's triumph in Cardiff meant he was now in possession of three of the four and one tantalizing step closer to achieving the Holy Grail of becoming the division's first man to hold the quartet at the same time.

Unsurprisingly Wilder's name was on everyone's lips inside the Principality Stadium from the moment the judges confirmed Joshua had outpointed Parker. The American had successfully defended his WBC title for the seventh time earlier in March, stopping Cuban Luis Ortiz in the 10th round in New York City, and even as AJ celebrated inside the ring, fans were calling for confirmation of a winner-takes-all fight that pundits agreed would smash box office records.

Wilder had turned down an invitation to watch Joshua fight Parker in Wales but despite his absence, AJ was quick to challenge the bronze medallist from the 2008 Beijing Olympics to go head-to-head.

"Are you asking me if I want to become undisputed champion of the world?" he said. "IBO, IBF, WBA, WBO – 21 professional fights, six world title fights. Does that not show how good I'm going? Forget the hype, I'm about business, let's get the business done. What would I have to do to beat Wilder? Get him in the ring and I knock him spark out."

The potential location of the fight proved a potential stumbling block, however, with Joshua insisting the American would have to come to the UK while Wilder was insistent the champion would have to defend his

three belts on the other side of the Atlantic in what would be AJ's first professional fight abroad.

"Everybody wants to see the fight," Wilder said. "The only people that don't are his promoters. They already know how big of a risk this really is. They should be worried but how long do they really think the public, the fans of boxing are going to allow them to stay away from me? This is the biggest fight in our era.

"Does he want to be remembered as a country-wide champion? Because he's not worldwide. Over here in America they don't even know his name. They just know him as a big guy from England. I need him and he needs me at the end of the day, unless he doesn't want to unify. Unless he wants to stay over his side of the pond and let people gravitate to him."

Whatever unfolds in the future inside the ring, Joshua will continue to be a busy man outside it, and he has made no secret that when the day does come to hang up his gloves he will be happy to swap the gym for the boardroom as he continues to build his business empire.

He took his significant first step towards this in 2015 when he set up "AJ Boxing and Commercial" to manage his sponsorship contracts and merchandise range. His blue chip sponsors include Jaguar Land Rover, Under Armour, Beats by Dre and Vodafone – and his relationship with these companies is all part of his ambitious plans for the future.

"When I first started boxing, the aim was to become a multimillionaire," he said in an interview with *GQ* magazine. "But now there are ordinary people, grandmas and granddads, who are worth millions just because of property prices. So the new school of thought is that I need to be a billionaire. Being a millionaire is good, but you have to set your sights higher. If I'm making £10 million from my next fight, my next target has to be making ten times that. And if I get to £100m–150m, why not go for the billion? I know self-made billionaires. It's hard, but it's possible."

Another arm to "AJ Boxing and Commercial" is the company's athlete management activities, and with the lure of working with Joshua, the department has already signed up two of British boxing's rising stars – 2016 Olympic light heavyweight champion Joshua Buatsi and unbeaten cruiserweight Lawrence Okolie, another of Team GB's fighters at the Rio Games.

AJ is also a shareholder in the exclusive BXR Gym in London, where he sometimes trains, and with his branded merchandise proving more popular with each fight, his business interests are going from strength to strength.

The combative nature of all successful boxers is part of AJ's DNA and in the build-up to the Parker fight, he admitted he could one day be tempted to swap the ring for the cage and try his hand at mixed martial arts.

"Providing I've got to the end of my career and achieved what I wanted to. Since the question was asked, I said, 'Yes, it would be an option because it's been done before and it's successful.' So it can be done again. I have to complete the goals and achievements I have in boxing otherwise it's like a pantomime. You have to dominate your own sport, and then you can look at other avenues."

Joshua's personal life looks certain to be equally frenetic going forward. He became a father to Joseph Bayley Temiloluwa Prince Joshua in late 2015 – born at Watford General Hospital – and he has admitted that fatherhood has given him a different perspective on the future.

"Before it was all about me," he said. "When he was born I thought I don't want to change because I'm very regimented but it's been a blessing. I lived for myself but then when I had my son, I started realizing there is someone who is going to be here after I'm gone and that's what he taught me, build something that they will respect and appreciate when I'm not here any more."

FOLLOWING PAGES:
Deontay Wilder's victory over Luis Ortiz in New York in March 2018 put the WBC champion on a collision course with AJ.

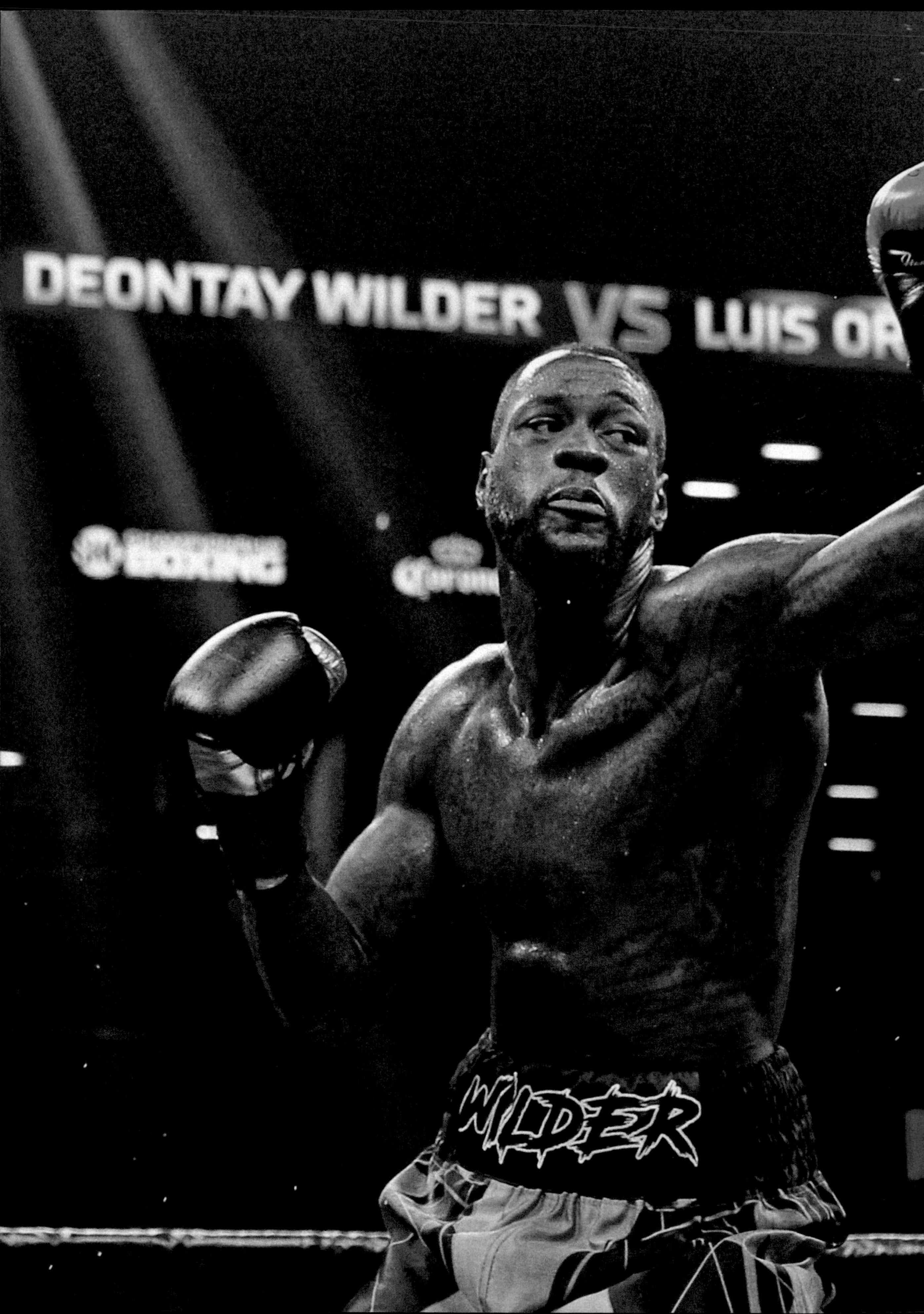
DEONTAY WILDER VS LUIS OR
WILDER

" I want to be the undisputed champion of the world. I do understand now, I have to play the game, if I want to create a legacy. I think I understand now, everything I have to gain and everything I have to do. I've never played a role. But look at the likes of Muhammad Ali, who became a sporting icon. Before I was happy to just be a part of boxing, and felt wherever I get to, it was always better than where I started. I never had a minute to reflect. But now I want to stamp my mark and my legacy and be among the likes of Federer. If I want to be considered like these guys, I have to carry myself the right way. I want to be like the Ronaldos, Messis and Federers. That's where I want to take boxing. "

AJ

CAREER
STATISTICS

Date	Venue	Opponent	Result	Details	Notes
20-Mar-10	London	Luke Herdman (GB)	Win	2nd-round stoppage	English ABA Elite National Championships
17-Apr-10	Bideford	Chris Duff (GB)	Win	Walkover	English ABA Elite National Championships
2-May-10	King's Lynn	Simon Hadden (GB)	Win	Walkover	English ABA Elite National Championships
14-May-10	London	Dominic Winrow (GB)	Win	1st-round stoppage	English ABA Elite National Championships
20-Jun-10	Alexandra Palace, London	Otto Wallin (SE)	Win	Points	Haringey Box Cup
30-Oct-10	Aldershot	Chris Devanney (IE)	Win	2nd-round stoppage	England v Ireland International
13-Nov-10	Manchester	Amin Isa (GB)	Win	Points 6:3	GB Amateur Boxing Championships
8-Dec-10	Wesport	Chris Turner (IE)	Win	Points 6:3	Ireland v England International
14-Jan-11	Stockholm	Otto Wallin (SE)	Win	Points 3:0	Sweden v England International
13-May-11	Colchester	Fayz Aboadi Abbas (GB)	Win	Points 24:15	English ABA Elite National Championships
18-Jun-11	Ankara, TR	Eric Brechlin (DE)	Win	Points 23:16	European Amateur Boxing Championships
20-Jun-11	Ankara, TR	Cathal McMonagle (IE)	Win	Points 22:10	European Amateur Boxing Championships

amateur career saw him rack up dozens of impressive performances. He quickly established himself as one of the most exciting young fighters on the scene

Date	Venue	Opponent	Result	Details	Notes
21-Jun-11	Ankara, TR	Mihai Nistor (RO)	Loss	3rd-round stoppage	European Amateur Boxing Championships
29-Sep-11	Baku, AZ	Tariq Abdul-Haqq (TT)	Win	3rd-round stoppage	AIBA World Boxing Championships
2-Oct-11	Baku, AZ	Juan Isidro Hiracheta (MX)	Win	1st-round stoppage	AIBA World Boxing Championships
4-Oct-11	Baku, AZ	Mohamed Arjaoui (MA)	Win	Points 16:7	AIBA World Boxing Championships
5-Oct-11	Baku, AZ	Roberto Cammarelle (IT)	Win	Points: 15:13	AIBA World Boxing Championships
7-Oct-11	Baku, AZ	Erik Pfeiffer (DE)	Win	1st-round stoppage	AIBA World Boxing Championships
8-Oct-11	Baku, AZ	Magomedrasul Medzhidov (AZ)	Loss	Points 21:22	AIBA World Boxing Championships
10-Feb-12	Debrecen, HUN	Sergey Kuzmin (RU)	Win	Points 9:7	Bocskai Memorial Tournament
11-Feb-12	Debrecen, HUN	Sardor Abdullayev (UZ)	Win	3rd-round stoppage	Bocskai Memorial Tournament
10-May-12	Kaunas, LTU	Sean Turner (IE)	Win	Points 9:5	Algirdas Socikas Tournament
11-May-12	Kaunas, LTU	Johan Linde (AT)	Win	1st-round knockout	Algirdas Socikas Tournament
12-May-12	Kaunas, LTU	Aidas Petruskevicius (LT)	Win	Walkover	Algirdas Socikas Tournament

STATISTICS

Date	Venue	Opponent	Result	Details
1-Aug-12	Excel, London	Erislandy Savon (CU)	Win	Points 17:16
6-Aug-12	Excel, London	Zhang Zhilei (CN)	Win	Points 15:11
10-Aug-12	Excel, London	Ivan Dychko (KZ)	Win	Points 13:11
12-Aug-12	Excel, London	Roberto Cammarelle (IT)	Win	Points 18:18 (count back)

for AJ to test himself against the best amateur fighters in the world. Olympic glory beckoned on the greatest of sporting stages

Date	Venue	Opponent	Result	Details
5-Oct-13	O2 Arena, London	Emanuele Leo (IT)	Win	1st-round stoppage
26-Oct-13	Motorpoint Arena, Sheffield	Paul Butlin (GB)	Win	2nd-round stoppage
14-Nov-13	York Hall, London	Hrvoje Kisicek (HR)	Win	2nd-round stoppage
1-Feb-14	Motorpoint Arena, Cardiff	Dorian Darch (GB)	Win	2nd-round stoppage

Turning pro did nothing to slow Joshua's ascent – as the numbers show with brutal clarity. The question wasn't whether AJ was ready to take on the world, it was whether the world was ready for him

Date	Venue	Opponent	Result	Details
1-Mar-14	SEEC, Glasgow	Hector Avila (AR)	Win	1st-round knockout
31-May-14	Wembley Stadium, London	Matt Legg (GB)	Win	1st-round knockout
12-Jul-14	Echo Arena, Liverpool	Matt Skelton (GB)	Win	2nd-round stoppage
13-Sep-14	Phones 4U Arena, Manchester	Konstantin Airich (DE)	Win	3rd-round stoppage

STATISTICS

Date	Venue	Opponent	Result	Details	Notes
11-Oct-14	O2 Arena, London	Denis Bakhtov (RU)	Win	2nd-round stoppage	Won vacant WBC International heavyweight title
22-Nov-14	Echo Arena, Liverpool	Michael Sprott (GB)	Win	1st-round stoppage	
4-Apr-15	Metro Radio Arena, Newcastle	Jason Gavern (US)	Win	3rd-round stoppage	
9-May-15	Barclaycard Arena, Birmingham	Raphael Zumbano Love (BR)	Win	2nd-round stoppage	
30-May-15	O2 Arena, London	Kevin Johnson (US)	Win	2nd-round stoppage	Retained WBC International heavyweight title
12-Sep-15	O2 Arena, London	Gary Cornish (GB)	Win	1st-round stoppage	Retained WBC International heavyweight title; won vacant Commonwealth heavyweight title
12-Dec-15	O2 Arena, London	Dillian Whyte (GB)	Win	7th-round knockout	Retained WBC International and Commonwealth heavyweight titles; won vacant British heavyweight title
9-Apr-16	O2 Arena, London	Charles Martin (US)	Win	2nd-round knockout	Won vacant IBF heavyweight title
25-Jun-16	O2 Arena, London	Dominic Breazeale (US)	Win	7th-round stoppage	Retained IBF heavyweight title
10-Dec-16	Manchester Arena	Eric Molina (US)	Win	3rd-round stoppage	Retained IBF heavyweight title
29-Apr-17	Wembley Stadium, London	Wladimir Klitschko (UA)	Win	11th-round stoppage	Retained vacant IBF heavyweight title; win vacant WBA (Super) and IBO heavyweight titles
28-Oct-17	Principality Stadium, Cardiff	Carlos Takam (FR)	Win	10th-round stoppage	Retained WBA (Super), IBF and IBO heavyweight titles
31-Mar-18	Principality Stadium, Cardiff	Joseph Parker (NZ)	Win	Unanimous points decision	Retained WBA (Super), IBF and IBO heavyweight titles, won WBO heavyweight title

Rising to the pinnacle of heavyweight boxing, AJ continues to rack up belts, titles and knockouts galore. And his astonishing run is far from over...

PICTURE
CREDITS

PREVIOUS PAGES:
Victory over Joseph Parker saw Anthony Joshua take a step closer to realizing his dream of becoming the first ever holder of all four major heavyweight world titles.

The publishers would like to thank the following sources for their kind permission to reproduce the pictures in this book.

Alamy: /Action Plus Sports Images: 80; /DPA Picture Alliance: 82, 115; /HFP Images: 118-119, 124, 130; /Scott Heavey: 9, 12-13, 107, 148-149; /Sport In Pictures: 35; /Adina Tovy: 50

Getty Images: 28, 31; /David M Benett: 142; /Charlie Crowhurst: 18BL; /Edward Diller/Icon Sportswire: 144-145; /Julian Finney: 135; /Stu Forster: 121; /John Gichigi: 18TR; /Richard Heathcote: 6-7, 11, 15, 104-105, 116, 123, 132, 136, 138-139, 141, 146, 156-157, 158-159; / Scott Heavey: 18TL, 54, 56, 58-59, 63, 65, 66-67, 69, 87, 88; /Dave J Hogan: 72; /Tom Jenkins: 96-97; / Stephen McCarthy/Sportsfile: 4; / Dan Mullan: 110; /Clive Rose: 37; / Mark Runnacles: 77; /Paul Thomas: 74-75, 81, 154-155; /Visionhaus/ Corbis: 2

REX/Shutterstock: 53; / Graham Chadwick: 32-33, 78; / Zsolt Czegledi/EPA: 27; /Alan Davidson/Silverhub: 36; /Matt Dunham/AP: 90-91, 102, 108; / Gareth Everett/Huw Evans: 129; /Chris Fairweather/Huw Evans: 126-127; /David Fisher: 62; / Paul Grover: 44; /Scott Heavey/ BPI: 46-47, 95; /Andy Hooper/ Associated Newspapers: 85; / Huw Evans Agency: 70; /Osman Karimov/AP: 20-21, 24, 150-151; /James Marsh/BPI: 112; / Geoff Pugh: 49; /Kevin Quigley/ Associated Newspapers: 61, 93, 100; /Dan Rowley: 43; /Dennis M Sabangan/EPA: 40-41; /Patrick Semansky/AP: 152-153; /Dave Shopland/BPI: 133; /Larry W Smith/EPA: 39; /TGSPhoto: 18BR; /Michael Zemanek/BPI: 99

Every effort has been made to acknowledge correctly and contact the source and/or copyright holder of each picture and Carlton Books Limited apologises for any unintentional errors or omissions, which will be, corrected in future editions of this book.

DK EYEWITNESS GUIDES

WHALE

The Dionysus Cup, ancient
Greek, c. 540 B.C.

Krill

Roman coin with
boy riding dolphin,
2nd century B.C.

17th-century engraving of whales
and whaling

Ancient Greek
bone figure of dolphin
with coral eye

Leaping killer
whale, or orca

Common dolphin

Dolphin-shaped
faience vase from
Rhodes, 550
to 500 B.C.

Female California
sea lion

EYEWITNESS GUIDES

Male walrus

WHALE

Written by
VASSILI PAPASTAVROU

Photographed by
FRANK GREENAWAY

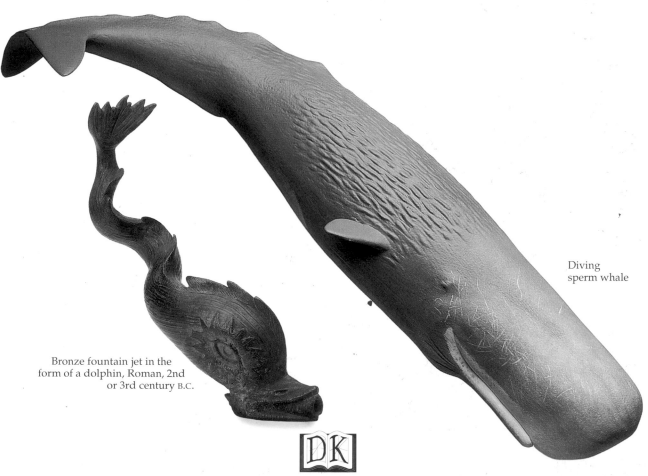

Diving
sperm whale

Bronze fountain jet in the
form of a dolphin, Roman, 2nd
or 3rd century B.C.

DK

DORLING KINDERSLEY
London • New York • Sydney • Moscow
www.dk.com

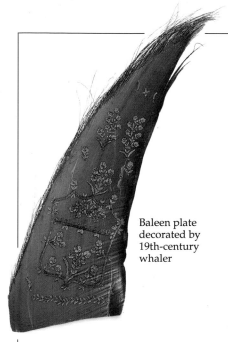

Baleen plate decorated by 19th-century whaler

Upper jaw of extinct whale *Basilosaurus*

Sperm whale tooth scrimshaw

A DORLING KINDERSLEY BOOK

www.dk.com

Project editor Scott Steedman
Art editor Bob Gordon
Managing editor Helen Parker
Managing art editor Julia Harris
Researcher Céline Carez
Picture research Sarah Moule
Production Catherine Semark
Live animals photographed at Marineland, Antibes, France and Harderwijk Marine Mammal Park, Holland
Editorial consultants Dr Peter Evans and Dr Paul Thompson

This Eyewitness ® Guide has been conceived by Dorling Kindersley Limited and Editions Gallimard

First published in Great Britain in 1993 by Dorling Kindersley Limited, 9 Henrietta Street, London WC2E 8PS

6 8 10 9 7

A CIP catalogue record for this book is available from the British Library.

ISBN 0 7513 6018 X

Colour reproduction by Colourscan, Singapore
Printed in China by Toppan Printing Co., (Shenzhen) Ltd

Whale meal

Spermaceti oil

Dyed baleen bristles

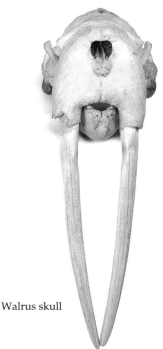

Walrus skull

Narwhal skull with long tusk

Gray whale

Contents

Marine mammals

AT FIRST SIGHT A DOLPHIN looks more like a fish than a person. But like you, the dolphin is a mammal, a warm-blooded animal that feeds its young on mother's milk. It is one of the many kinds of whale, the most successful group of marine mammals. Several other unrelated groups of mammals, including seals and dugongs, also make their homes in salt water. Millions of years ago their ancestors left the land to live in the sea. Over time they evolved to suit their new environment, becoming sleek and streamlined. Unlike fish, which take oxygen from the water, marine mammals must come to the surface regularly to breathe. But taking oxygen from the air is efficient, and most marine mammals are fast swimmers and powerful hunters.

ARISTOTLE
Whales are mammals, not fish. The Greek scientist and philosopher Aristotle recognized this 2,400 years ago. He also noticed that they suckle their young and breathe air, like other mammals.

GLOBE SWIMMERS
This globe made from an ostrich egg shows whales swimming all over the world. Marine mammals live in every ocean, from the balmy tropics to the icy polar seas, and in several great rivers. Some migrate vast distances to feed and give birth.

WHALE SIZED
In every language, whale means "big"! Even the smallest whales are the size of a person. This pilot whale weighs 1,300 kg (2,850 lb), about 18 times more than an adult man. The largest whales are bigger than any dinosaur and the blue whale, the largest of all, weighs 200 tonnes and is as long as a Boeing 737 jet!

Layer of fur protects and keeps animal warm

FIN FOOT
Seals, sea lions, and walruses are all pinnipeds, which means "fin footed". They are powerful swimmers superbly adapted to life in the sea. As their name suggests, they have webbed feet. But unlike whales, they have not lost their back legs and have to come ashore to give birth.

Powerful front flippers used to propel sea lion through water

SEA MONSTER
Whales are mysterious creatures. The biggest species live far out to sea and spend most of their lives under water. Early drawings were based on sailors' stories of sea monsters with huge mouths that huffed and puffed like dragons.

Webbed back flippers

Dorsal fin

Blow-hole

WHALES AND DOLPHINS
Of all marine mammals, the best adapted to life in the sea are the cetaceans, or whales. The group gets its name from the Greek word *ketos*, meaning "sea monster". It includes dolphins and porpoises, which are really whales. This bottlenose dolphin is a typical whale. It is a powerful swimmer with strong tail flukes, two pectoral (chest) fins, a dorsal (back) fin, and no hind legs. It breathes through a blow-hole on the top of its head.

Pectoral fins, used to steer while swimming

Tough, rubbery skin with very few hairs

Swimming muscles that drive the whale through water

Flukes, the correct name for a whale's "tail"

THAR SHE BLOWS!
No group of animals has been hunted as ruthlessly as whales (pp. 46–51). They were once common in all the world's oceans, but by the middle of this century many populations had been virtually wiped out. The industry declined, and a public outcry helped to control the killing. But many whale populations may never recover (p. 63).

Light colour blends in with snow and ice of Arctic

SEA SIRENS
Like whales, manatees and dugongs have no hind legs and spend their entire lives in the water (pp. 44–45). They are gentle vegetarians, and sailors used to mistake them for mermaids. They are known as sirenians, from the Greek word for mermaid, *seiren*.

SEA BEAR
Are polar bears marine mammals? Probably, because they depend on the sea. For much of the year, polar bears live on the floating ice pack, spending hours in the water hunting seals. They are superb swimmers but cannot stay under water very long.

Heavy coat of fur keeps bear warm

SEA OTTER
Most otters are found in rivers, but there are two species that live all the time in salt water. Sea otters entered the oceans relatively recently and are not as well adapted as other marine mammals. They are sleek and streamlined, with dense fur and webbed feet.

Powerful paws used to kill prey such as seals

Whale evolution

THE FIRST MAMMALS all lived on land. How or why the ancestors of whales returned to the sea is still unclear. About 55 million years ago, a group of mammals seem to have colonized salty estuaries teeming with fish. Over the millennia, they gradually changed to suit their watery home. Skulls of early whales show how their nostrils moved to the top of the head to make breathing under water easier. Strong tail flukes for swimming evolved, front limbs turned into blades for steering, and back limbs slowly wasted away. Baleen whales have developed a different way of feeding (pp. 24–25), but they probably share the same ancestors as toothed whales. One clue is that they are born with tiny tooth buds that never develop.

AN EARLY WHALE?

Most scientists agree that whales have the same ancestors as even-toed ungulates (hoofed animals), which include modern cows and deer. These ancestors lived on land and hunted other animals. This is a model of *Mesonyx*, an odd carnivore that looked like a wolf but had hooves like a cow. Just like today's carnivores, *Mesonyx* had several different kinds of teeth (pp. 22–23).

OLD WHALE

The *archæocetes* (Latin for old whales) lived in shallow seas and salty estuaries 55 million years ago. Their nostrils were still at the front of their heads.

Nostrils near front of snout

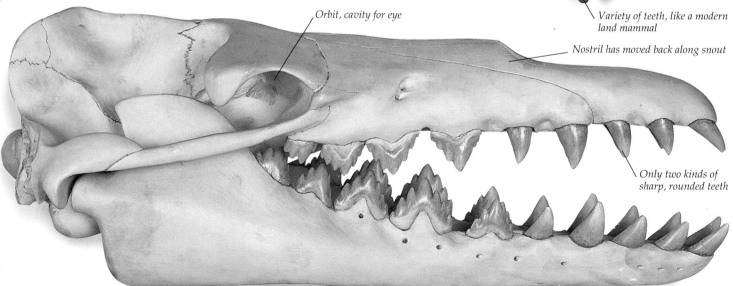

Orbit, cavity for eye

Variety of teeth, like a modern land mammal

Nostril has moved back along snout

Only two kinds of sharp, rounded teeth

SEAFOOD PLATTER

We know almost nothing about how early whales lived. But the teeth give some clues. *Prozeuglodon isis* probably lived in shallow water, where it caught fish and ground up shells to eat the soft-bodied animals within.

MORE LIKE A DOLPHIN

In some ways the skull of *Prosqualodon davidi*, which lived 25 million years ago, looks like a modern dolphin's skull (p. 23). Its blow-hole must have been near the top of its head, and its teeth are all a similar size and shape.

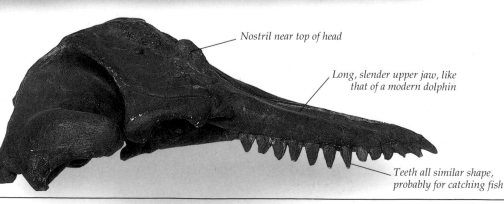

Nostril near top of head

Long, slender upper jaw, like that of a modern dolphin

Teeth all similar shape, probably for catching fish

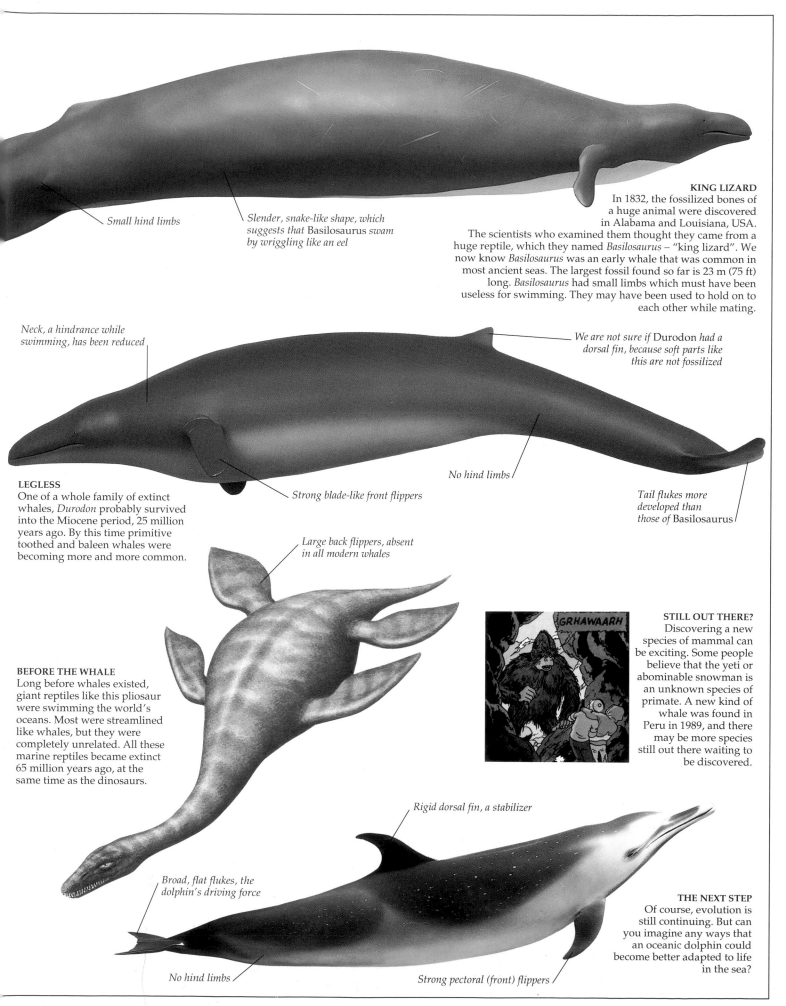

Small hind limbs

Slender, snake-like shape, which suggests that Basilosaurus *swam by wriggling like an eel*

KING LIZARD
In 1832, the fossilized bones of a huge animal were discovered in Alabama and Louisiana, USA. The scientists who examined them thought they came from a huge reptile, which they named *Basilosaurus* – "king lizard". We now know *Basilosaurus* was an early whale that was common in most ancient seas. The largest fossil found so far is 23 m (75 ft) long. *Basilosaurus* had small limbs which must have been useless for swimming. They may have been used to hold on to each other while mating.

Neck, a hindrance while swimming, has been reduced

We are not sure if Durodon *had a dorsal fin, because soft parts like this are not fossilized*

LEGLESS
One of a whole family of extinct whales, *Durodon* probably survived into the Miocene period, 25 million years ago. By this time primitive toothed and baleen whales were becoming more and more common.

Strong blade-like front flippers

No hind limbs

Tail flukes more developed than those of Basilosaurus

Large back flippers, absent in all modern whales

BEFORE THE WHALE
Long before whales existed, giant reptiles like this pliosaur were swimming the world's oceans. Most were streamlined like whales, but they were completely unrelated. All these marine reptiles became extinct 65 million years ago, at the same time as the dinosaurs.

STILL OUT THERE?
Discovering a new species of mammal can be exciting. Some people believe that the yeti or abominable snowman is an unknown species of primate. A new kind of whale was found in Peru in 1989, and there may be more species still out there waiting to be discovered.

GRHAWAARH

Rigid dorsal fin, a stabilizer

Broad, flat flukes, the dolphin's driving force

THE NEXT STEP
Of course, evolution is still continuing. But can you imagine any ways that an oceanic dolphin could become better adapted to life in the sea?

No hind limbs

Strong pectoral (front) flippers

9

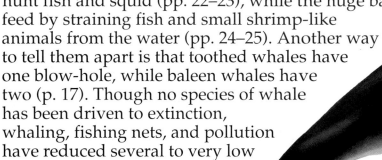

BOTTLENOSE DOLPHIN
Star of the TV show *Flipper*
(p. 54), this is the whale most
people know best.

Whales big and small

WHALES ARE FOUND IN EVERY OCEAN, from the tropics to the icy waters of the Poles, and in five of the world's greatest rivers. At a maximum length of 31 m (109 ft) and weight of 200 tonnes, the blue whale is the largest animal that has ever lived. At the other end of the scale, the smallest dolphins and porpoises are less than 2 m (6 ft) long, the size of an adult person. There are about 78 species of whale, in two main groups. The toothed whales like the dolphins and the sperm whale hunt fish and squid (pp. 22–23), while the huge baleen whales like the blue and fin whales feed by straining fish and small shrimp-like animals from the water (pp. 24–25). Another way to tell them apart is that toothed whales have one blow-hole, while baleen whales have two (p. 17). Though no species of whale has been driven to extinction, whaling, fishing nets, and pollution have reduced several to very low numbers (pp. 58–59).

Harbour porpoise
North Atlantic Ocean
To 1.8 m (6 ft)

No beak

THE PORPOISE FAMILY
All six species of porpoise are small, with a maximum length of little more than 2 m (6 ft). They have no beak, and can be easily identified from close examination by their spade-shaped teeth. Dall's porpoise lives in deep ocean waters, but the other five stick close to the coast.

*Row of bumps
instead of dorsal fin*

OCEAN-GOING DOLPHINS
The largest family of whales, dolphins thrive in every ocean except the cold waters of the Arctic and Antarctic. Most of the 26 species have a similar shape, but some do not have an obvious beak, and two have no dorsal fin. Their distant relatives the river dolphins are found in the fresh waters of the Yangtze, Amazon, Indus, and Ganges rivers (p. 33).

Dorsal fin curves like a sickle

Prominent beak

Most dolphin species can be identified by the distinctive patterns on their flanks

Scratches from collisions with boats and encounters with sharks and killer whales and of course from each other

Common dolphin
Oceans and seas worldwide
To 2.4 m (8 ft)

Powerful tail flukes

THE NARWHAL FAMILY
The unicorn of the seas, the male narwhal has one of the most remarkable teeth of any animal (pp. 36–37). Like its close relative the beluga, it lives in the icy waters of the Arctic. The third member of this family, the Irrawaddy dolphin, is found far away in tropical Asia. Unlike most other whales, all three species have unfused neck vertebrae, which allow them to turn their heads.

Narwhal
Arctic seas
To 4.7 m (15 ft 5 in)

BEAKED WHALES
These are the most mysterious whales. Of the 18 species, one has never been seen alive and is known only from two skulls washed up on the beach. Another species was first reported in 1989. The beaked whales are all creatures of the open ocean, where they are thought to feed on squid far below the surface. Females have no visible teeth, while males usually have one pair on their protruding lower jaws.

Dorsal fin far back on body

Cuvier's beaked whale
Oceans worldwide
To 7 m (23 ft)

Sperm whale
Oceans worldwide
To 18.5 m (60 ft)

SPERM WHALES
The great sperm whale is the largest toothed whale. With its huge, square head and massive teeth, it is hard to confuse with any other animal. It was immortalized by Herman Melville in his novel *Moby Dick* (p. 38). Like the killer whale, the sperm whale is found all over the world. Its two cousins, the pygmy and dwarf sperm whales, are much smaller and are restricted to tropical and temperate waters.

Colonies of barnacles and lice live on skin and may cause scars

Gray whale
North Pacific Ocean
To 15 m (50 ft)

Melon, probably used in echo-location to find squid

BALEEN WHALES
Gentle filter-feeders, the baleen whales include the biggest animals on Earth. There are three families: the right whales, the gray whale, and the rorquals. The four species of right whales have smooth bellies with no throat grooves and large mouths that hold long, narrow plates of baleen. The gray whale is unusual enough to be placed in a family of its own. It was once found in the Atlantic Ocean, but whalers had exterminated this population by the 18th century.

Fin whale
Oceans worldwide
To 24 m (78 ft)

Long-finned pilot whale
Atlantic and Pacific
To 8.5 m (28 ft)

KILLERS AND PILOTS
These six whales have blunt heads with no beaks and few teeth. The best known species, the killer whale or orca, grows to 9 m (30 ft) long and is found all over the globe (pp. 34–35). Little is known about the smaller species, including the pygmy killer, little bigger than a porpoise.

THE MIGHTY RORQUALS
The rorquals are the real giants of the animal kingdom. The largest of the six species, the blue whale, is the size of a jet airliner. The smallest, the minke, reaches a mere 10 m (33 ft). With the exception of the humpback, rorquals are thin, sleek beasts that move surprisingly fast – up to 50 km/h (30 mph). They can be identified by their throat grooves, which allow their throats to expand and gulp vast quantities of water.

11

Inside the whale

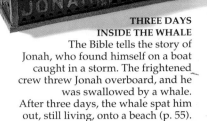

LIKE ITS OUTSIDES, a whale's insides are enormous. A blue whale's arteries are as big as drainpipes and its heart is the size of a small car. Its huge tongue weighs 4 tonnes. Whales have all the same internal organs as other mammals, but many have been modified to cope with life in the sea. For example, they have huge kidneys, which they need to get rid of excess salt. Whales have no hind limbs. But many species have a few vestigial (left-over) back leg bones, reminders of their ancestors that walked on land (pp. 8–9). Baleen whale skeletons are easily identified by their vast mouths, which allow the whales to gulp enormous quantities of seawater (pp. 24–25).

BIG MOUTH
The biggest mouth in the animal kingdom belongs to the blue whale. The huge jaw bones are sometimes erected as arches. This one in the old whaling port of Whitby, England, comes from one of the last blue whales ever caught (pp. 20–21).

THREE DAYS INSIDE THE WHALE
The Bible tells the story of Jonah, who found himself on a boat caught in a storm. The frightened crew threw Jonah overboard, and he was swallowed by a whale. After three days, the whale spat him out, still living, onto a beach (p. 55).

Lumbar (back) vertebrae

Tall processes, where powerful swimming muscles join the backbone

Chevrons, V-shaped bones attached to bottom of vertebrae

Sacral (pelvic) vertebrae

Caudal (tail) vertebrae

Porpoise flipper

Scapula

Humerus

Radius

Ulna

Metacarpals

Wrist bone

Phalanges

Scapula (shoulder blade)

SMELLY BONES
In 1830, visitors flocked to the Royal College of London to admire the bones of a huge right whale. Mounting skeletons of this size is a difficult engineering feat. Many of the bones are too heavy for one man to carry, and have to be held in place by strong steel girders. Whale bones contain a lot of oil and are very smelly before they are cleaned.

Humerus (upper arm bone)

A WHALE'S ARM
A person's arm and a porpoise's flipper look very different on the outside. But under the skin are the same bones, adapted over the millennia to their different functions. A human arm is long and thin, designed for climbing or carrying and manipulating objects. The porpoise's flipper, used for steering and braking, is much shorter and stronger.

Human arm

Ulna

Radius

Wrist bones

Metacarpals (Hand bones)

Phalanges (Finger bones)

SPONGY BONE
A land mammal's entire weight is held up by its bones, which are hard and strong. But the great weight of a whale is supported by the sea, and its bones have become soft and spongy. This can be clearly seen in Inuit carvings of whale bones, like this sculpture of a seal.

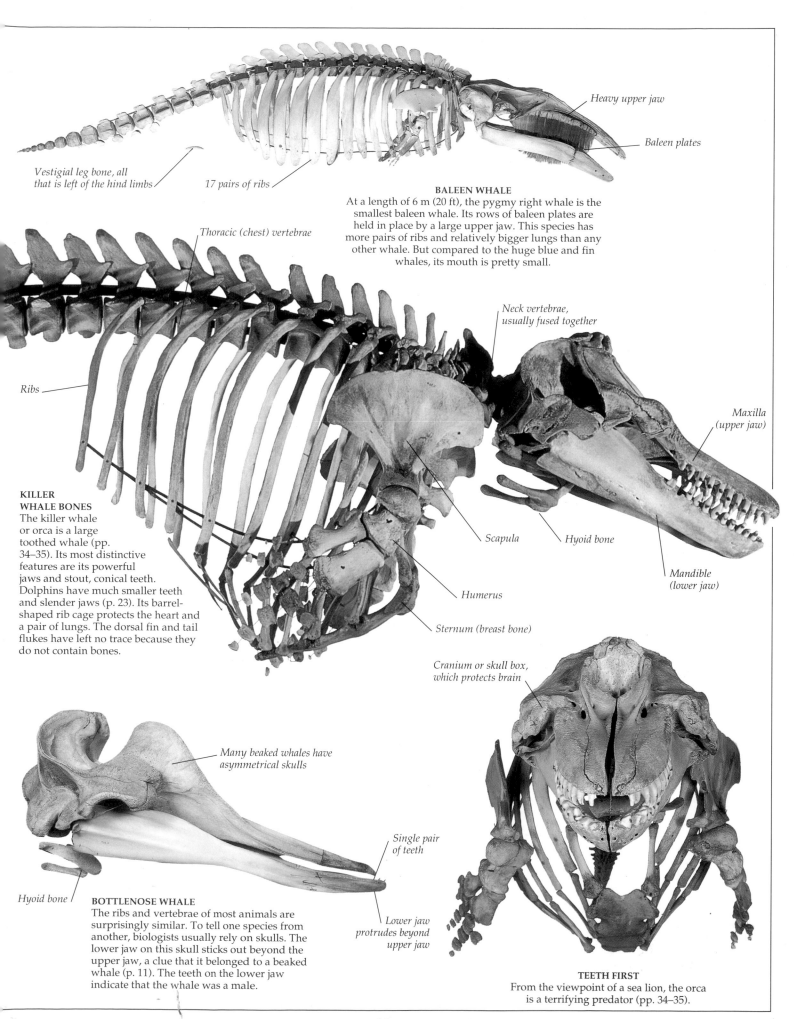

Heavy upper jaw

Baleen plates

Vestigial leg bone, all
that is left of the hind limbs

17 pairs of ribs

BALEEN WHALE
At a length of 6 m (20 ft), the pygmy right whale is the
smallest baleen whale. Its rows of baleen plates are
held in place by a large upper jaw. This species has
more pairs of ribs and relatively bigger lungs than any
other whale. But compared to the huge blue and fin
whales, its mouth is pretty small.

Thoracic (chest) vertebrae

Neck vertebrae,
usually fused together

Maxilla
(upper jaw)

Ribs

**KILLER
WHALE BONES**
The killer whale
or orca is a large
toothed whale (pp.
34–35). Its most distinctive
features are its powerful
jaws and stout, conical teeth.
Dolphins have much smaller teeth
and slender jaws (p. 23). Its barrel-
shaped rib cage protects the heart and
a pair of lungs. The dorsal fin and tail
flukes have left no trace because they
do not contain bones.

Scapula

Hyoid bone

Mandible
(lower jaw)

Humerus

Sternum (breast bone)

Cranium or skull box,
which protects brain

Many beaked whales have
asymmetrical skulls

Single pair
of teeth

Hyoid bone

BOTTLENOSE WHALE
The ribs and vertebrae of most animals are
surprisingly similar. To tell one species from
another, biologists usually rely on skulls. The
lower jaw on this skull sticks out beyond the
upper jaw, a clue that it belonged to a beaked
whale (p. 11). The teeth on the lower jaw
indicate that the whale was a male.

Lower jaw
protrudes beyond
upper jaw

TEETH FIRST
From the viewpoint of a sea lion, the orca
is a terrifying predator (pp. 34–35).

Seals and sea lions

ALL IN THE FAMILY
The largest seal, the male elephant seal, grows to 6.5 m (21 ft) and weighs more than four tonnes. The smallest species, the ringed and Baikal seals, still reach 1.37 m (4 ft 6 in) and weigh 64 kg (140 lb).

HAULED OUT
Seals come onto land or ice to give birth. This is called hauling out. Land-breeding seals like the elephant seal gather at a few popular beaches, where competition between bulls (males) can be intense. Bigger, stronger bulls usually triumph, so bulls are usually much bigger than cows (females). Ice-breeding seals like this ringed seal are spread out over a larger area, and bulls and cows are closer to the same size.

ALL 34 SPECIES OF SEAL are hunters. Most feed on fish, but some, such as the ferocious leopard seal, eat other seals. There are three families: the true or earless seals (18 species), the eared seals (15 species), and the walrus, which is unusual enough to go in a family of its own. Seals are found all over the world, but they are most common in the icy waters of the Arctic and Antarctic. This is probably because food supplies are more reliable there than in warmer waters. Many species have been reduced to low numbers by human activities. Sealing was just as ruthless as whaling (pp. 52–53), and millions of animals were killed in the last two centuries. Now other seal populations are seriously threatened by pollution (pp. 58-59). Seals spend much of their lives at sea, where they are hard to study. Yet new techniques like satellite tracking (p. 61) are revealing surprising new things about this remarkable and mysterious group of mammals.

TRUE SEALS
This common or harbour seal is a true seal. It has a round, chubby shape and no obvious ear flaps. Like all true seals, it cannot turn its hind flippers under its body, so it cannot climb very well on land. But it moves surprisingly fast on rocky shores. This family includes the world's most common marine mammal, the crabeater seal, and the monk seals, which are among the rarest.

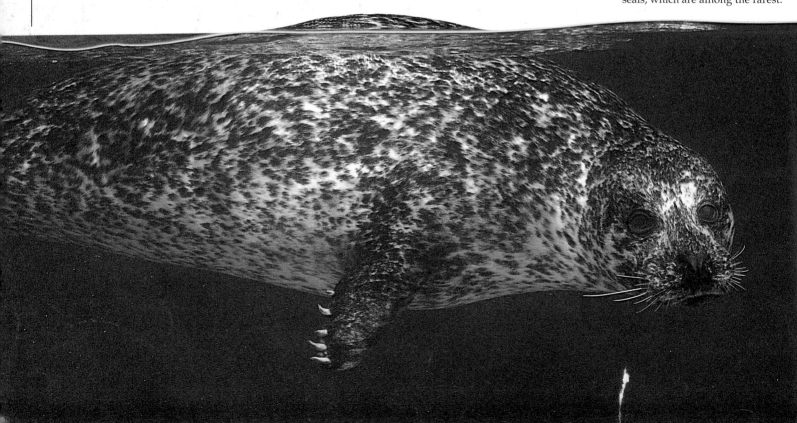

Sensitive whiskers

A COUPLE OF WALRUSES
Walruses live around the moving ice pack of the northern oceans (pp. 42–43). Bulls are about 50 per cent heavier than cows. Both sexes are kept warm by a thick blanket of blubber that can make up half of their body weight. Unlike whales, they are quite hairy, with bushy whiskers to help them find their prey in the dark and murky depths.

COLD COMFORT
In the Arctic, the native Inuit (Eskimo) people have always hunted seals for their meat, fur, and hides (p. 52). They even use seal tendons and bones to make tools or rope. This Inuit stone carving of a seal comes from Frobisher Bay in the Canadian Arctic.

Female or cow walrus

Front flippers steer while swimming

Male or bull walrus

Thick layer of blubber for warmth and protection

Cribbage board carved from a walrus tusk and decorated with seals

WATER HOUNDS
Biologists think seals evolved from dog-like carnivores and share the same ancestors as this jackal. But why did they take to the sea 30 million years ago? Probably because changes in ocean currents created rich new food supplies in the oceans.

EARED SEALS
Like all eared seals, this California sea lion is using its long front flippers to swim through the water; true seals and walruses push with their hind flippers instead (p. 19). There are two main groups of eared seals, the sea lions and the fur seals. They have longer limbs than true seals, and are more agile on land. Like most seals they have large eyes to help them navigate and find prey under water.

Suited to life in the sea

WHALES AND SEALS ARE SUPERBLY SUITED to life in the sea. Because they are supported by the water, they do not need strong legs, and have evolved a sleek shape that slides easily through the water. Many species can swim as fast as a small boat. Powerful muscles in the tail and flanks drive them forwards. Their fins are also streamlined, like a plane's wings. Water is a cold home, and almost all whales and seals have thick layers of blubber which keep them very warm. Many seals also have heavy, oily fur which traps bubbles of air and keeps the animals warm and dry.

DIVING IN
In most of the world, the ocean is cold enough to take your breath away. In polar seas, a human would barely survive a minute. Water is a very good conductor of heat, so an animal loses heat 25 times faster in water than in the air.

Long guard hairs

Fine underfur

A LINED COAT
A close look at a fur seal's coat reveals two kinds of hair. The longer, thicker hairs protect the seal as it scrapes against the rocks. But it is air bubbles caught in the fine, dense underfur that keep the seal warm.

SUN BATHING
Seals and sea lions often bask in the sun to warm up. But they are so well insulated that they can easily get too hot. When this happens, they cool off by waving their front flippers in the air or burying them in the sand. When northern elephant seals overheat, they flip cool sand over their backs (pp. 40–41).

Female California sea lion

Male California sea lion

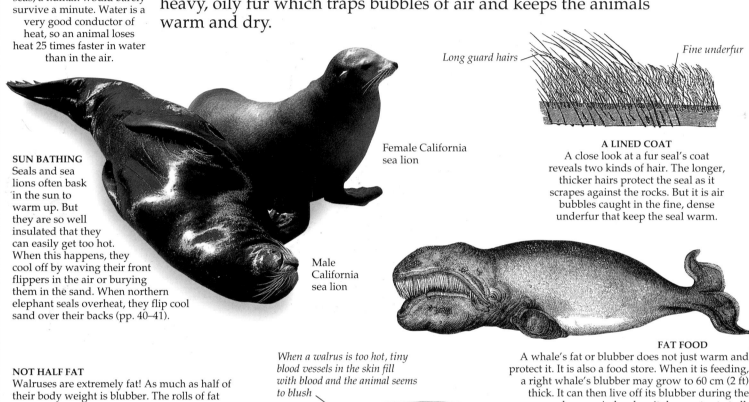

FAT FOOD
A whale's fat or blubber does not just warm and protect it. It is also a food store. When it is feeding, a right whale's blubber may grow to 60 cm (2 ft) thick. It can then live off its blubber during the long periods when it does not eat at all.

NOT HALF FAT
Walruses are extremely fat! As much as half of their body weight is blubber. The rolls of fat keep them warm in the freezing seas and ice floes of the Arctic. Thousands of walruses were once killed for their blubber, which was boiled and turned into oil. (p. 53).

When a walrus is too hot, tiny blood vessels in the skin fill with blood and the animal seems to blush

KEEPING YOUR HEAD ABOVE WATER
Humans are poor swimmers. They have no flippers or tail flukes, and get cold because they have hardly any fat. They can barely hold their breath for more than a minute, and have to stick their mouths out of the water to gulp air. Whales have solved all these problems. They have even evolved blow-holes that allow them to breathe through the top of the head.

OPEN...
A whale's blow-hole is a modified nostril that sits on top of its head. Toothed whales like this orca only have one blow-hole. This opens so the whale can snort the old air out of its huge pair of lungs.

Massive, broad pectoral fin

... AND CLOSED
Muscles force the blow-hole shut before the orca submerges.

Coming up to breathe

Taking a breath at sea is a difficult business. Underwater, a whale's blow-hole or a seal's nostrils are shut tight. When the whale surfaces, it breathes out very rapidly. The "blow" forms a fine mist of spray up to 4 m (13 ft) high that can be seen kilometres away. A moment later, the whale breathes in and submerges. Seals breathe out and dive with empty lungs.

DOUBLE-BARRELLED
Baleen whales have two blow-holes that sit side-by-side. Their blow usually looks like a single spray of mist. Only right whales produce distinctive double blows. This minke whale's blow is almost invisible, except in the very coldest Antarctic waters.

Umbilicus (belly button)

Genital slit

Anus

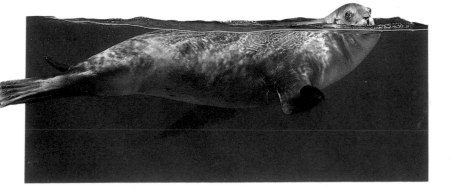

SEAL SOLUTIONS
A seal's eyes and nostrils are at the top of its head, so they stick out of the water while it swims along. Seals and sea lions can even sleep at sea. Some species sleep underwater and somehow manage to wake up every few minutes to breathe. Other kinds of seal sleep at the surface with their nostrils poking out of the water like a snorkel. This is called bottling.

TORPEDO SHAPED
Land animals come in all shapes and sizes. This is because they move in air, which hardly provides any resistance. But swimming through water is hard work, and marine animals all have a similar, stream-lined shape. Even their sexual organs, which would slow them down, are tucked away in a genital slit.

17   *Continued on next page*

Long pectoral fin or flipper

Throat grooves, a clue that
the humpback is a rorqual

ON A WING AND A SONG
This leaping humpback is showing off its
graceful flippers, much longer than any
other whale's. These are way too long for
simple steering, and are sometimes used to rub
other whales. Humpbacks also slap their flippers
on the water, to make loud splashing noises. This is
called flippering.

TICKET TO RIDE
Barnacles make their homes on the skin of slow-
moving whales such as right and gray
whales. Rorquals like the blue whale
are too fast for most hangers-on.
Sperm whales are slow, but they
regularly shed huge sheets of
dead skin. This makes it hard
for other animals to hitch a
free ride for long

Finding their way around

Whales and seals live in a world that is very different
from our own. Even in the clearest ocean water
visibility is rarely more than 30 m
(100 ft), and they have to hunt at
night or in murky water. Seals
rely on sensitive whiskers.
Toothed whales have
developed a system of echo-
location, using sounds to
find food and their way
around (pp. 26–27). How
whales navigate when they
migrate thousands of
kilometres is another question.
They may have a special magnetic
sense and a built-in compass.

Ear flap

Nose like a dog's

Large eyes

Long whiskers,
specialized hairs used
in close quarters

EYEBALL TO EYEBALL
In the murky ocean, eyes are less use than on
land. This gray whale's eyes are not much
larger than a cow's. They must be pretty
useless while the whale is feeding on the
muddy ocean bottom. But gray whales spy
hop – stick their heads out of the water
to have a look around.

These muscles contract
to pull tail up

Upstroke begins

Upstroke

Downstroke begins

HEAD FULL OF SENSES
For their size, seals have much bigger eyes than whales. Their
senses are similar to a dog's. Apart from the walrus (pp. 42–43),
seals can all see well in and out of the water. This California sea
lion has large eyes and good vision even in dim light.
Its nose is very dog-like. The long whiskers are especially
useful in dark or murky waters.

FISHY TAIL
A fish's tail is vertical, not
horizontal like a whale's. It moves
its tail from side to side to swim.

These muscles
contract to pull tail down

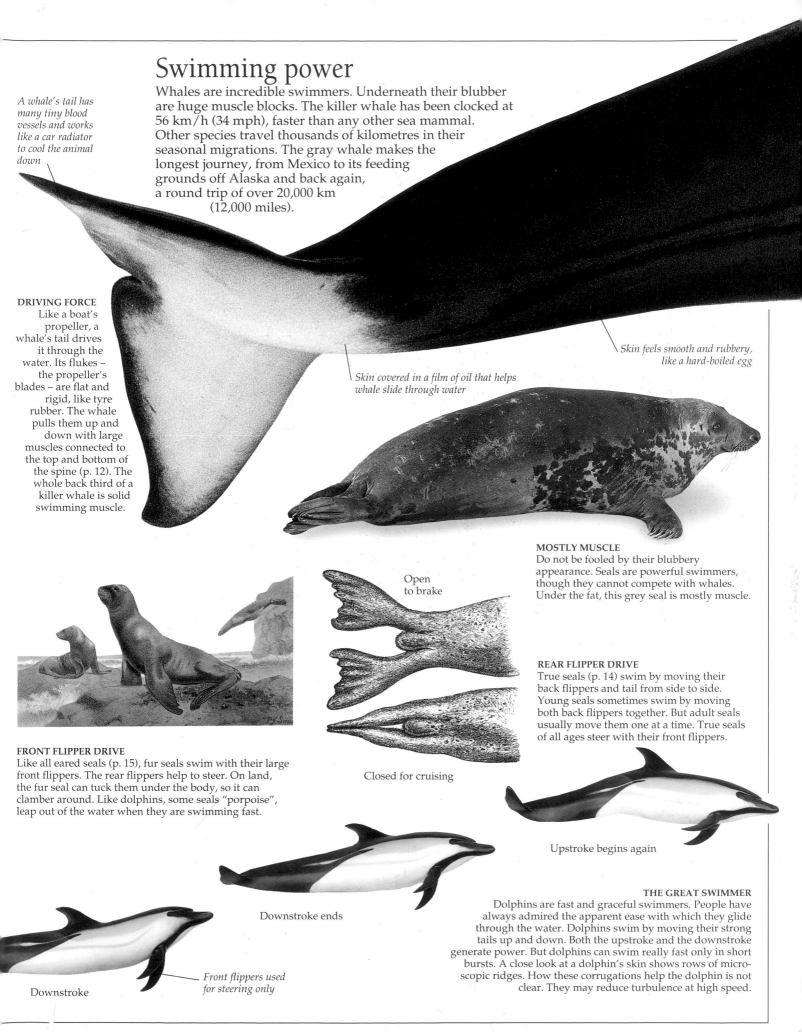

Swimming power

Whales are incredible swimmers. Underneath their blubber are huge muscle blocks. The killer whale has been clocked at 56 km/h (34 mph), faster than any other sea mammal. Other species travel thousands of kilometres in their seasonal migrations. The gray whale makes the longest journey, from Mexico to its feeding grounds off Alaska and back again, a round trip of over 20,000 km (12,000 miles).

A whale's tail has many tiny blood vessels and works like a car radiator to cool the animal down

DRIVING FORCE
Like a boat's propeller, a whale's tail drives it through the water. Its flukes – the propeller's blades – are flat and rigid, like tyre rubber. The whale pulls them up and down with large muscles connected to the top and bottom of the spine (p. 12). The whole back third of a killer whale is solid swimming muscle.

Skin covered in a film of oil that helps whale slide through water

Skin feels smooth and rubbery, like a hard-boiled egg

MOSTLY MUSCLE
Do not be fooled by their blubbery appearance. Seals are powerful swimmers, though they cannot compete with whales. Under the fat, this grey seal is mostly muscle.

Open to brake

REAR FLIPPER DRIVE
True seals (p. 14) swim by moving their back flippers and tail from side to side. Young seals sometimes swim by moving both back flippers together. But adult seals usually move them one at a time. True seals of all ages steer with their front flippers.

FRONT FLIPPER DRIVE
Like all eared seals (p. 15), fur seals swim with their large front flippers. The rear flippers help to steer. On land, the fur seal can tuck them under the body, so it can clamber around. Like dolphins, some seals "porpoise", leap out of the water when they are swimming fast.

Closed for cruising

Upstroke begins again

Downstroke ends

THE GREAT SWIMMER
Dolphins are fast and graceful swimmers. People have always admired the apparent ease with which they glide through the water. Dolphins swim by moving their strong tails up and down. Both the upstroke and the downstroke generate power. But dolphins can swim really fast only in short bursts. A close look at a dolphin's skin shows rows of microscopic ridges. How these corrugations help the dolphin is not clear. They may reduce turbulence at high speed.

Downstroke

Front flippers used for steering only

Ocean giants

THE BIGGEST WHALE – and the biggest animal that has ever lived – is the blue whale. Only other baleen whales and the sperm whale come anywhere near its enormous size. The largest living land animal, the bull elephant, could stand on a blue whale's tongue! Even the biggest dinosaur weighed less than a quarter of a large blue whale. Such size has its benefits. Big animals are less likely to be attacked by predators, and it is easier for them to keep warm. The big problem is finding enough food to nourish their awesome bulk.

Pectoral fin

Tail flukes

WHALE LICE
A number of animals make their homes on the great expanse of a whale's skin. Some are harmless hangers-on, but others, like this whale louse, probably irritate the skin.

TALL TAIL
Unlike some baleen whales, blue whales raise their tails in the air when they dive.

Stubby dorsal fin

A WHALE OF A SHARK
It is no coincidence that whale sharks, the world's largest fish, are also filter feeders. Because animals that feed on plankton do not need to chase individual prey, they do not have to be agile. This has allowed some to grow to great sizes. Whale sharks do not have baleen plates. Instead, they filter food from the water with their gills.

THE WORLD'S BIGGEST BABY
The day it is born, a baby blue whale is already as big as an elephant. It has no baleen plates, and relies entirely on its giant mother's milk. Like seal milk, this is very high in fat. Every day the growing whale drinks about 100 litres (175 pints) of milk and puts on another 90 kg (200 lb). By the time it is weaned, after six or seven months, the young blue whale is already 16 m (54 ft) long.

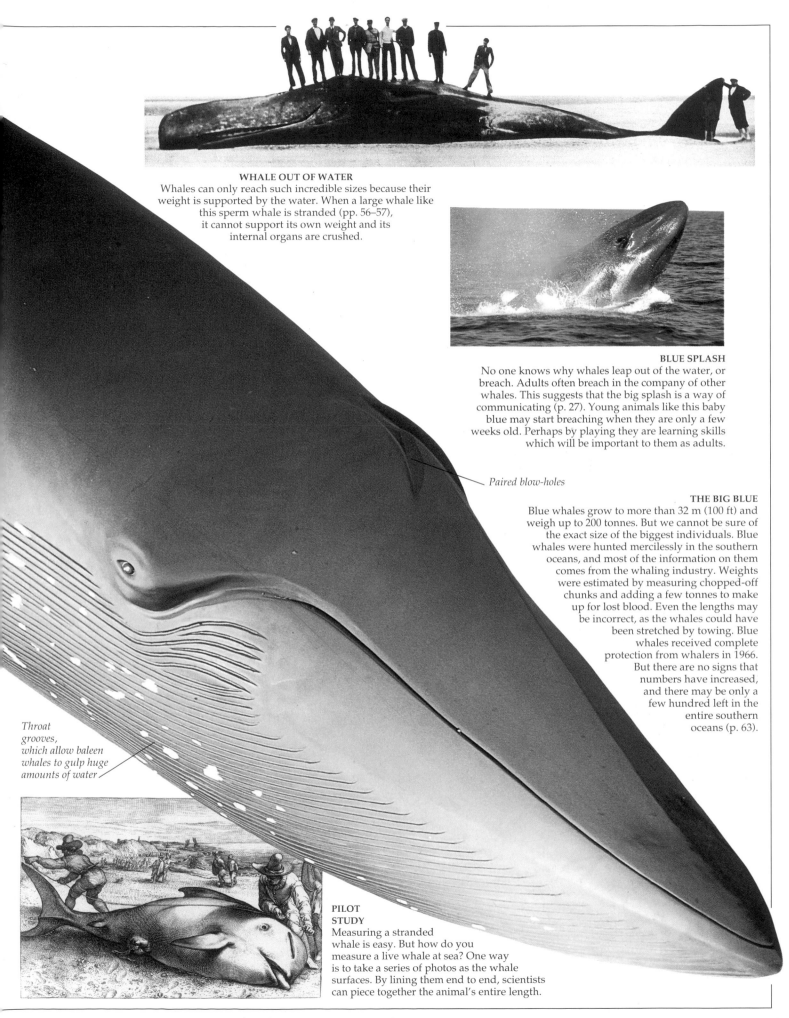

WHALE OUT OF WATER
Whales can only reach such incredible sizes because their weight is supported by the water. When a large whale like this sperm whale is stranded (pp. 56–57), it cannot support its own weight and its internal organs are crushed.

BLUE SPLASH
No one knows why whales leap out of the water, or breach. Adults often breach in the company of other whales. This suggests that the big splash is a way of communicating (p. 27). Young animals like this baby blue may start breaching when they are only a few weeks old. Perhaps by playing they are learning skills which will be important to them as adults.

Paired blow-holes

THE BIG BLUE
Blue whales grow to more than 32 m (100 ft) and weigh up to 200 tonnes. But we cannot be sure of the exact size of the biggest individuals. Blue whales were hunted mercilessly in the southern oceans, and most of the information on them comes from the whaling industry. Weights were estimated by measuring chopped-off chunks and adding a few tonnes to make up for lost blood. Even the lengths may be incorrect, as the whales could have been stretched by towing. Blue whales received complete protection from whalers in 1966. But there are no signs that numbers have increased, and there may be only a few hundred left in the entire southern oceans (p. 63).

Throat grooves, which allow baleen whales to gulp huge amounts of water

PILOT STUDY
Measuring a stranded whale is easy. But how do you measure a live whale at sea? One way is to take a series of photos as the whale surfaces. By lining them end to end, scientists can piece together the animal's entire length.

Teeth for grasping…

MYSTERY TOOTH
Only mature male sperm whales have teeth. These are huge, up to 25 cm (10 in) long. How females and young males manage to feed and what males use their teeth for are both mysteries.

Mᴏsᴛ ᴡʜᴀʟᴇs ᴀɴᴅ sᴇᴀʟs are hunters that catch their slippery prey with rows of sharp teeth. Like most meat-eating mammals (including people), seals and sea lions have a range of different teeth. They grasp their food with powerful canines and incisors and then chew it up with premolars and molars. But toothed whales have simple, peg-like teeth that are all the same shape. Teeth are also used for fighting. One of the most amazing teeth of all, the male narwhal's tusk, is probably used to establish dominance over other males (pp. 36–37). Some beaked whales have teeth that are so strangely shaped that it is hard to imagine what they are for (p. 13)! Perhaps the simple sight of the male's huge teeth makes him irresistible to female whales.

ATLANTIC MACKEREL
Dolphins and seals eat a wide range of fish, from bottom-dwelling cod to fast mackerel like this one. Many dolphins hunt co-operatively.

LEOPARD OF THE SEAS
Leopard seals are fierce predators that feed on penguins and even other species of seal. They also strain krill through their teeth, like crabeater seals (p. 25).

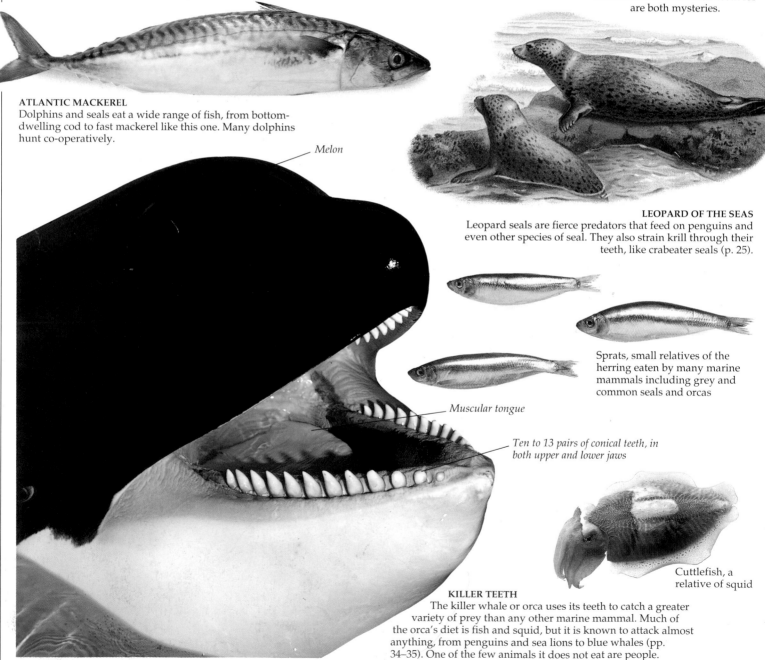

Melon

Muscular tongue

Ten to 13 pairs of conical teeth, in both upper and lower jaws

Sprats, small relatives of the herring eaten by many marine mammals including grey and common seals and orcas

Cuttlefish, a relative of squid

KILLER TEETH
The killer whale or orca uses its teeth to catch a greater variety of prey than any other marine mammal. Much of the orca's diet is fish and squid, but it is known to attack almost anything, from penguins and sea lions to blue whales (pp. 34–35). One of the few animals it does not eat are people.

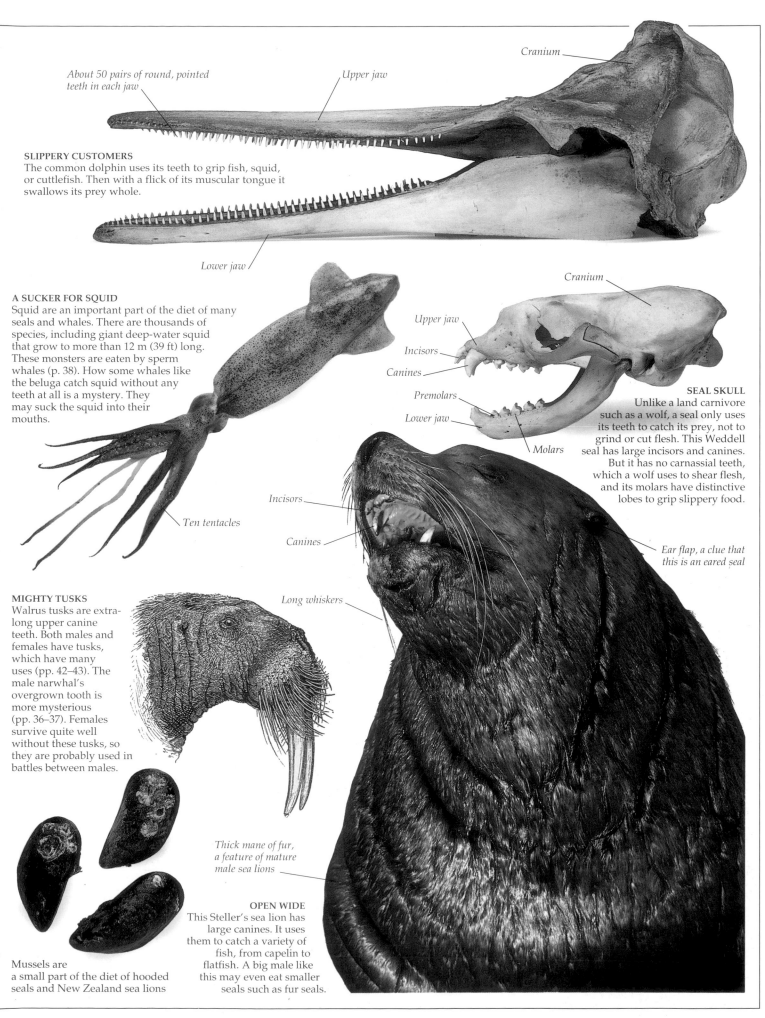

Cranium

Upper jaw

About 50 pairs of round, pointed teeth in each jaw

SLIPPERY CUSTOMERS
The common dolphin uses its teeth to grip fish, squid, or cuttlefish. Then with a flick of its muscular tongue it swallows its prey whole.

Lower jaw

A SUCKER FOR SQUID
Squid are an important part of the diet of many seals and whales. There are thousands of species, including giant deep-water squid that grow to more than 12 m (39 ft) long. These monsters are eaten by sperm whales (p. 38). How some whales like the beluga catch squid without any teeth at all is a mystery. They may suck the squid into their mouths.

Ten tentacles

Cranium

Upper jaw

Incisors

Canines

Premolars

Lower jaw

Molars

SEAL SKULL
Unlike a land carnivore such as a wolf, a seal only uses its teeth to catch its prey, not to grind or cut flesh. This Weddell seal has large incisors and canines. But it has no carnassial teeth, which a wolf uses to shear flesh, and its molars have distinctive lobes to grip slippery food.

Incisors

Canines

Ear flap, a clue that this is an eared seal

MIGHTY TUSKS
Walrus tusks are extra-long upper canine teeth. Both males and females have tusks, which have many uses (pp. 42–43). The male narwhal's overgrown tooth is more mysterious (pp. 36–37). Females survive quite well without these tusks, so they are probably used in battles between males.

Long whiskers

Thick mane of fur, a feature of mature male sea lions

Mussels are a small part of the diet of hooded seals and New Zealand sea lions

OPEN WIDE
This Steller's sea lion has large canines. It uses them to catch a variety of fish, from capelin to flatfish. A big male like this may even eat smaller seals such as fur seals.

... and baleen for filtering

SOME OF THE BIGGEST WHALES feed by filtering. Their filters are baleen plates, huge fringed brushes that hang inside their mouths like giant sieves. The three families of baleen whales have evolved different filtering techniques. But they all draw seawater into their mouths and spit it back out through the baleen, trapping any tasty morsels on the inside. Some feed mainly on krill, small shrimp-like animals found in huge numbers in the southern oceans. Others gulp down entire schools of fish. Most baleen whales pack a whole year's feeding into four or five summer months. In this time their weight may increase by 40 per cent. Much of the energy is stored as fat in preparation for the long migrations to winter breeding grounds (p. 19).

ANOTHER FILTERER
Like whales, flamingos are filter feeders. They have fringed beaks quite similar to baleen plates which they skim through the mud upside-down.

BIG GULP
Rorquals have throat grooves which allow them to expand their mouths to engulf huge quantities of water. A blue whale can take in 60 tonnes of water in one gulp. Then the whale forces the water out by closing its mouth and contracting the grooves. Anything too large to pass through the baleen filter is trapped on the inside and swallowed.

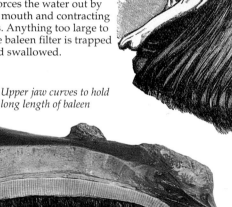

RAISING THE CURTAINS
The right whale's huge head contains 200 to 270 pairs of baleen plates. These hang from the whale's upper jaw like two great curtains with the fringes facing inwards.

Blow-hole

Upper jaw curves to hold long length of baleen

Section cut away to show baleen plates with fringes facing inside mouth

Massive lower lip

Callosities, areas of rough, horny skin infested with barnacles and lice

The right whale's head can make up a quarter of its body length

SKIMMERS AND GROVELLERS
Right whales usually feed by swimming slowly along with lips parted. Water flows in the front and out the sides of the mouth. Unlike rorquals, they do not open their mouth very wide, but their high, curved lips can hold much longer baleen plates. These are protected by huge lower lips, up to 5 m (16 ft) high in large individuals. The gray whale, the other kind of baleen whale, swims along the bottom making troughs in the mud like a bulldozer. Bowhead whales, a kind of right whale, have been seen feeding in both ways.

Hard outer edge

Inner fringe

FIN WHALE BALEEN
Like your hair and fingernails, baleen is made of a substance called keratin. It grows continually, replacing the fringe as it is worn away.

FINE FILTER
A right whale's baleen grows to 4.3 m (14 ft), much longer than any other whale's. The extremely fine hairs can trap very small animals.

Top attaches to whale's upper jaw

FITTING TOGETHER
Baleen plates grow from ridges like the ones you can feel on the roof of your mouth. They fit together like cards in a deck.

Baleen plate decorated by 19th-century whaler

KRILL
Krill are shrimp-like creatures no longer than your finger. In the summer they occur in enormous swarms that can cover kilometres of the southern oceans, where they are the main food for most baleen whales.

Fine fringe where prey is trapped

Incisors

Canines

Cheek teeth with three lobes trap krill in mouth

SIEVING SEAL
Despite its name, the crabeater seal does not eat crabs! Instead it uses its strangely shaped teeth to filter krill from the water. This unusual tactic must be successful, because there are more crabeater seals in the world than any other species of seal.

Upper jaw of first whale

Upper jaw of second whale

Baleen plate

BLOWING BUBBLES
In some parts of the world, humpback whales use bubbles to herd fish together. This is known as bubble netting. The whale swims in a spiral under the fish, blowing bubbles all the time. Then with its mouth wide open it surfaces in the middle and gulps down the whole school. Humpbacks feed alone or in groups of up to 25 animals. These two are fishing together in the cold waters of the Antarctic.

Lower jaw of first whale, bulging with water and fish

Clicks, barks, and songs

SOUND TRAVELS WELL in water, and the seas are noisy places. Whales and seals live in a world dominated by sound. Dolphins co-ordinate their hunts with whistles and clicks, and male humpbacks sing to attract females. Most large whales make sounds by slapping the surface or breaching – leaping out of the water and coming down with a splash. These splashes can be heard for kilometres and are probably a kind of communication. The most sophisticated use of sound is in echo-location. Only toothed whales and bats have perfected this skill. By sending out a pulse of sound and listening to the returning echo, whales can find their way around and locate fish and squid in the dark water. The biggest toothed whale, the sperm whale, may even stun squid with loud clicks (pp. 38–39). Baleen whales also make loud sounds. Early sailors were terrified when they heard strange rumbles and groans through the hulls of their wooden ships. Like a lot of things whales do, we are just beginning to understand these low-frequency calls, which may travel hundreds of kilometres through the seas.

EAR BONE
From the outside, a small pinprick is the only sign of a whale's ear. This dense bone is part of a baleen whale's inner ear.

SIGNATURE WHISTLE
Every dolphin makes its own, unique whistle. Scientists listen to these "signature whistles" to identify individuals. Mothers and their calves have similar-sounding whistles.

WHISTLING WALRUS
Seals that mate in the water make elaborate underwater sounds. Among the noisiest of all are male walruses courting females. Their songs include loud gongs, like underwater bells. They also rise out of the water to bark, whistle, growl, and clack their teeth.

HUMPBACK HITS
Humpback whales are the only non-humans to get into the music charts. Many people enjoy listening to the soothing sounds of humpbacks, belugas, and killer whales. A recording of humpback songs was put aboard the *Voyager* space probe as a greeting from Planet Earth.

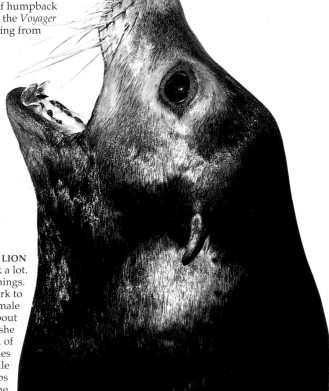

LOVE SONG
The male humpback whale sings a beautiful, haunting song for hours on end. All alone, he sings floating motionless in the water with his head hanging down. Like a lot of male birds, humpbacks sing to attract females. The song consists of a number of phrases repeated over and over again. Each individual sings his own song, slightly different from any other, which evolves slowly from year to year. Whales from different areas sing distinctive themes, so scientists can tell which population a whale comes from by its song.

BARKING SEA LION
Seals and sea lions bark a lot. A bark can have many meanings. Male California sea lions bark to frighten off other males. If a female elephant seal (pp. 40–41) is about to be mated by a small male, she will bark to attract the attention of the dominant male, who rushes over and chases the small male away. Seal mothers and pups bark to find each other on the crowded beach (p. 31).

MOBY CLICK
When sperm whales get together, they often repeat slow patterns of clicks, called codas. When one whale produces a particular coda, another will repeat it in turn. Sperm whales have huge brains (pp. 38–39). But it is hard to imagine that they can say anything very complicated with such simple clicks.

Two-tonne killer whale or orca

WAILING IT OUT
When famous Italian opera singer Luciano Pavarotti sings, he is forcing air past vocal cords that vibrate in his throat. The air leaves through his mouth, so he has to pause every few seconds to breathe in. But whales have no vocal cords, and humpbacks can warble for half an hour between breaths. To do this they must be able to recycle air. Some dolphins can even whistle and echo-locate at the same time.

OUT OF THE WATER...
Why do whales breach? The loud splashes can be heard many kilometres away, and are probably a way of communicating. Whales probably slap the water with their tails (lobtailing, p. 38) or flippers (p. 18) for the same reason.

...AND DOWN WITH A SPLASH!
Whales are more likely to breach when they are with other whales, and humpbacks breach more in rough weather than calm. This may be the only way to make themselves heard above the water noise.

Melon, a waxy bulge in the forehead which may be a lens to focus sounds

Blow-hole

Lower jaw may be used to receive echo

Clicks produced in nasal sacks, bulges in nasal tubes below blow-hole

Echoes "heard" through inner ear, where lower jaw meets skull

SOUND SENSATION
Dolphins produce trains of clicks for echo-location. These can sound like buzzes or doors creaking. But don't be fooled by this open mouth – dolphins produce sounds in nasal sacks beneath their blow-holes. Echo-location is an incredibly precise sense. Blindfolded, dolphins can still find objects or tell between two balls of slightly different sizes. They may also make loud bangs to stun fish.

Courtship and birth

THE URGE TO REPRODUCE is strong, and takes up a lot of a whale or seal's time and energy. Seals risk the danger of coming ashore to find a mate and give birth. In many species of whale and seal, the males compete for females, with the winning (dominant) males mating with many females. In these species, the males are usually bigger than the females. The most amazing example of this is the elephant seal, where big males are ten times bigger than females (pp. 40–41). Whales and seals usually mate and give birth in the spring, so their pregnancies last a year. Most seals have a pup every year, while many species of whale only raise one calf every three or even ten years.

THE RIGHT STUFF
In winter, southern right whales gather in shallow bays to mate. Several males mate with each female, one after another. The only way a female can escape is by plunging her head under water and sticking her tail in the air. The males just wait, because they know that sooner or later she will have to take a breath.

ICE BREEDER
A seal's link with land may be brief. Common seals are born at low tide and swim off before the tide is high again. This hooded seal has a huge choice of ice floes to haul out on, so females are not crowded into a small area. Males are usually seen with only one female at a time. But each female is probably mated by several males, one after another.

TUSK, TUSK!
There is usually a lot of bluffing and counterbluffing when males compete. In most species, full-blown fights are rare. These male walruses are fighting for a spot in the water close to a herd of females. A lot is at stake. The winner may mate with more than a dozen females; the loser may never mate at all.

Female walrus, identified by her smaller size and darker colour

A walrus pregnancy lasts 15 to 16 months, longer than any other seal's

LOVE IN A COLD CLIMATE
Walruses have a long and intimate courtship. Males seduce females with barks, growls, and haunting whistles (p. 26). A female who is impressed by his love song will slip off with a male. This female (left) and male (right) are rubbing moustaches. Each female only mates with one male. Mating takes place in the water.

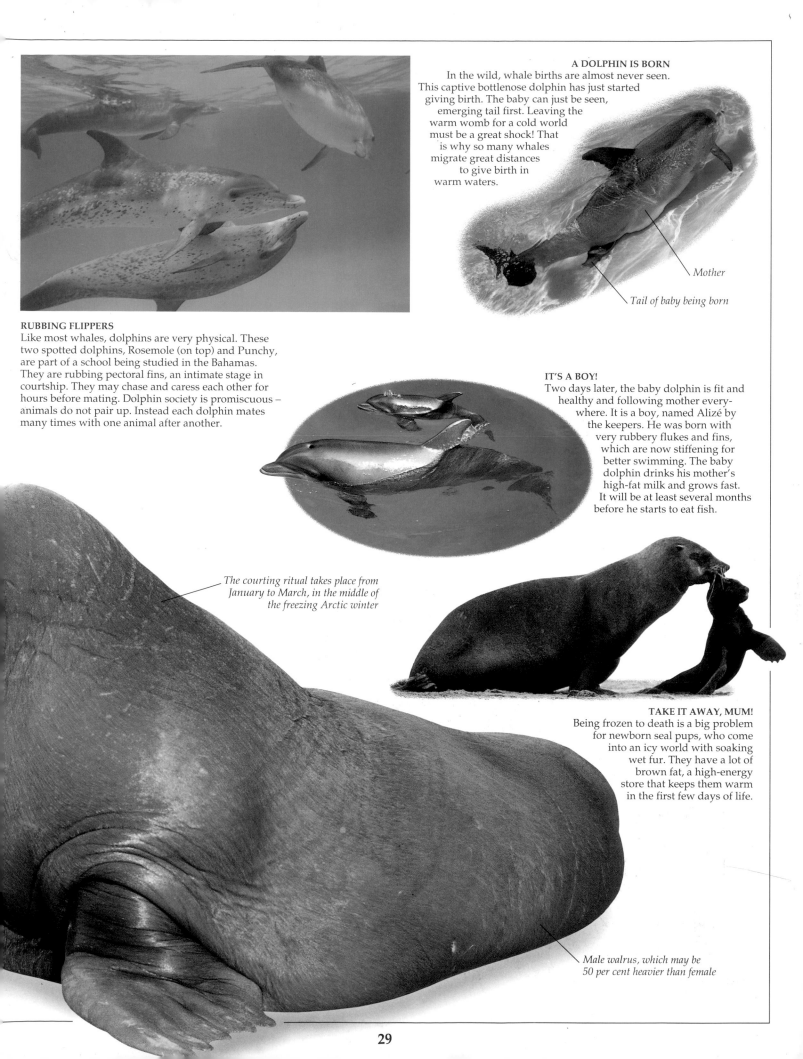

A DOLPHIN IS BORN
In the wild, whale births are almost never seen. This captive bottlenose dolphin has just started giving birth. The baby can just be seen, emerging tail first. Leaving the warm womb for a cold world must be a great shock! That is why so many whales migrate great distances to give birth in warm waters.

Mother

Tail of baby being born

RUBBING FLIPPERS
Like most whales, dolphins are very physical. These two spotted dolphins, Rosemole (on top) and Punchy, are part of a school being studied in the Bahamas. They are rubbing pectoral fins, an intimate stage in courtship. They may chase and caress each other for hours before mating. Dolphin society is promiscuous – animals do not pair up. Instead each dolphin mates many times with one animal after another.

IT'S A BOY!
Two days later, the baby dolphin is fit and healthy and following mother every-where. It is a boy, named Alizé by the keepers. He was born with very rubbery flukes and fins, which are now stiffening for better swimming. The baby dolphin drinks his mother's high-fat milk and grows fast. It will be at least several months before he starts to eat fish.

The courting ritual takes place from January to March, in the middle of the freezing Arctic winter

TAKE IT AWAY, MUM!
Being frozen to death is a big problem for newborn seal pups, who come into an icy world with soaking wet fur. They have a lot of brown fat, a high-energy store that keeps them warm in the first few days of life.

Male walrus, which may be 50 per cent heavier than female

Social life

THE SOCIAL LIVES of marine mammals are as varied as the animals themselves. Many seals spend the mating season crowded together on beaches (pp. 28–29). Some whales live alone; others like killer whales spend their whole lives in a small group of close relatives (pp. 34–35). Living in a group protects against attack and allows animals to share in the care of young. Many species of whale also hunt in groups, co-operating to round up fish or even attack other whales or seals (pp. 34–35). Planning and executing complex behaviour like this takes intelligence, and whales seem to be extremely clever. Whales and dolphins are playful and learn new tasks quickly. But does this make them intelligent? It is hard to judge, because our world is so different from theirs.

FIGHTING FOR A SPOT
Good spots for seals and sea lions to come ashore are few and far between. They prefer remote islands and sandbanks, far away from predators such as wolves, bears, or people. So beaches are crowded with aggressive males and females nursing young pups.

SWIMMING LESSONS
Like many young whales, this humpback calf swims close to mother and is pulled along almost effortlessly in her slipstream. The bond between mother and young is very strong in all mammals. Many whales drink mother's milk for several years. A young whale has a lot to learn. Even taking a breath takes some practice, and newborn whales often bob right out of the water. But with a little help from mother, they soon learn to surface gracefully.

FATHER AND SON?
This Steller's sea lion pup is resting on the back of a huge male, who may be its father. Neither the pup nor the male can know for sure. Because of this uncertainty, male seals have little to do with family life beyond mating with females.

DANCE OF THE DOLPHINS

Dolphin societies are complex and difficult for people to observe. The warm, shallow waters of the Bahamas are one of the few places in the world where schools can be studied over long periods. These spotted dolphins live in schools of fifty or more. Like other social animals, dolphins have disagreements and conflicts. They often confront each other head to head, squawking with open mouths. These conflicts rarely end in physical injury.

THE DAILY STRUGGLE

These Steller's sea lions are fighting over a fish. During the day, groups of about fifty sea lions have been seen heading out to sea. They work together to find and herd schools of fish or squid. At night, the sea lions usually hunt alone.

SUCKLING SEA LION

This female Steller's sea lion is many times smaller than the male below. She is suckling a young pup. The breeding beaches are so crowded that pups are often crushed when the huge males rush over to mate with females. A female leaves her pup regularly to go fishing. So how does she tell her pup from the hundreds of others on the beach when she gets back? She starts by making a warbling call which attracts any pups nearby. Then she smells and touches any likely-looking youngsters until she is sure she has found hers.

Female sperm whale rolling upside-down

Calf

Female sperm whale

Female rolling upside-down

COMMUNAL BABYSITTING

Because whales live so long, studying their family lives takes decades. Such studies have only just begun, and little is known about most species. We know that female sperm whales live together in big groups with their young calves (p. 39). Males only spend a few hours with each family group every year. One of the females in this group is probably the mother of the small calf. The other females may be sisters or aunts. When the mother dives deep under water to feed, another female will babysit the calf, protecting it from sharks or killer whales.

Dolphins and porpoises

PEOPLE HAVE LONG been fascinated by the graceful dolphin. Imagine the magical sight of a school of dolphins leaping for the sheer fun of it, or bow riding, cruising effortlessly on the pressure waves of a boat. The ocean-going dolphins and their close relatives the porpoises are common in all the world's oceans (except for the coldest polar seas). There is still discussion about how the 60 or more species are related. Some species number in the millions and are found all over the world. Others are limited to tiny areas, which makes them more vulnerable. A few species have been reduced to very low numbers by human activity (pp. 58–59). So far, no species has become extinct, and there may just be time to save the two most at risk, the Mexican harbour porpoise (vaquita) and the Chinese river dolphin (p. 63).

PORPOISING
Leaping into the air while swimming along is called porpoising. Strangely enough, most porpoises never do it! The one exception is Dall's porpoise.

LE DAUPHIN
The eldest son of the king of France was given the title *Le Dauphin*, French for "The Dolphin". The title was first adopted by the lords of Viennois, France, who had three dolphins on their coat of arms. When his father died, *Le Dauphin* became king. What happened to the last *Dauphin*, the son of Louis XVI, is still a mystery. His father was executed in 1793, during the French Revolution.

Tail flukes with a central nick, like virtually all whales

WITH TIME ON HIS SIDE
Almost nothing is known about the hourglass dolphin, which gets its name from the pretty black-and-white pattern on its sides. Though they are not shy and often bow ride, they are usually found far out to sea in the remote waters of the southern oceans.

FISHY TAILS
The ancient Minoans and Greeks were fascinated by dolphins, which were much more common in the Mediterranean Sea in their day. Many Greek myths and legends feature dolphins (pp. 54–55). Like most sea-farers, Greek sailors were happy to see dolphins playing near their boats. These animals come from the great palace of Knossos on the island of Crete. They are about 3,500 years old. The fresco painter has given them vertical tails, so they look more like fish than dolphins.

ACROBAT
Dusky dolphins are great leapers. They are coastal animals that live off New Zealand, southern Africa, and South America. Off Peru they are hunted in large numbers for their meat.

Hump instead of dorsal fin

BOTTLENOSE DOLPHIN
Different populations of the same species can look very distinct. The bottlenose dolphin is one of the biggest and most common dolphins, found in all kinds of habitat from shallow coastal waters to the deep ocean. Coastal dolphins are smaller and often stay in a particular area. Oceanic animals grow over 4 m (13 ft) long and wander widely.

RIVER DOLPHIN
Some dolphins have pink patches, but only the Amazon River dolphin is pink all over (p. 63). Like the four other species of river dolphin, it has a long beak studded with many teeth. In the murky rivers where these dolphins live, eyes are virtually useless. They rely instead on echo-location to find fish to eat. It is still unclear if the five river dolphins are closely related. They may have just evolved similar solutions to the problems of river life.

Small eyes – some species of river dolphin are completely blind

Long beak

Big flippers for steering

Coin from Tarentum showing Taras, son of the Greek god of the sea Poseidon, on a dolphin, 331–302 B.C. (pp. 54–55)

Distinctive beak, a feature of dolphins but not of porpoises

Broad, curving flippers

JUMP FOR JOY
Porpoising is an efficient way to take a breath without slowing down. One way of calculating how fast a dolphin swims is to measure how high it leaps. To jump 5.5 m (18 ft) up, a dolphin would have to break the surface at 36 km/h (22 mph). But dolphins do not just leap for practical reasons. They also seem to jump for the sheer fun of it!

SPOTTED SCHOOL
Spotted dolphins have long, slender bodies and pronounced beaks. They are very similar to their close relatives the striped and spinner dolphins. Like most species, they live in schools and have complex social lives that we are barely beginning to understand (pp. 30–31).

Tall, sickle-shaped dorsal fin

BITTEN AND SCARRED
Risso's dolphins are squid eaters. They are found in all but the coldest waters of the Indian, Pacific, and Atlantic oceans. Risso's is the only species of dolphin that has no beak. They live in big groups and are constantly scratching and biting each other. Old animals are almost white with thousands of criss-cross scars.

Scars from bites

Long, curving flippers

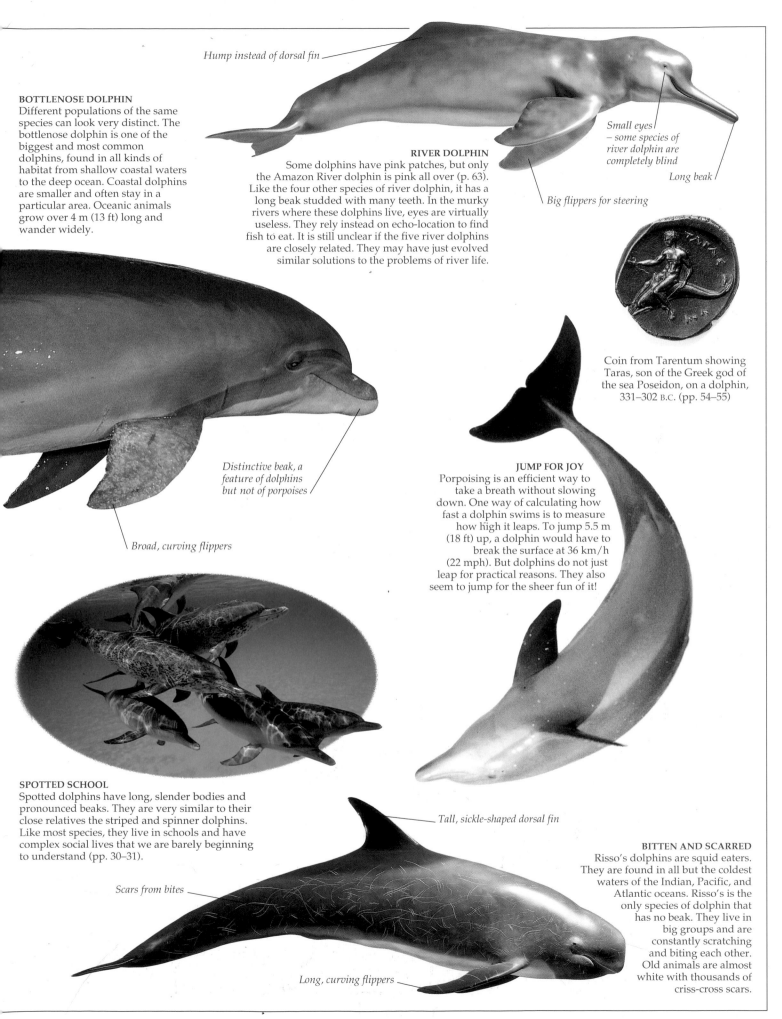

The killer whale

THERE IS NO MISTAKING an orca or killer whale, with its tall dorsal fin, rounded head and startling black-and-white pattern. An adult male can be 9 m (30 ft) long and weigh 10 tonnes. Most of this is muscle, for the orca is the fastest mammal in the seas (p. 19), sprinting at up to 56 km/h (34 mph). This awesome hunter eats almost everything, from small fish to great whales ten times its size. Its ferocious appetite gave it the common name, killer whale. Orcas have no natural predators. Until the 1960s, they were feared and sometimes shot. But opinions have changed, partly because orcas do not seem to eat humans. Orcas are long-lived – a female may reach 90 years old. But they reproduce very slowly, with a calf about every eight years. They live in tight social groups called pods. They hunt co-operatively, and seem to be highly intelligent. Pods of orcas have been seen working together to herd salmon or tip a seal off an ice floe.

FALSE KILLER
Like the two kinds of pilot whale, this false killer whale is a close relative of the orca. False killers are black all over. They swim with a slow, lazy action. They are the largest whales to bow ride, hitching a free swim from the waves made by boats (p. 32). False killers occasionally eat other marine mammals.

GIANT KILLERS
Imagine the struggle between a great whale and a pod of killers. Even a huge blue whale has no chance against such an attack. Orcas have been seen organizing attacks on all sorts of whales, including a whole pod of sperm whales.

Eye

White patch, not eye!

Rounded flippers are black top and bottom

Stiff dorsal fin

White belly

WHY ARE THEY BLACK AND WHITE?
The jet black and shocking white may help to camouflage a killer whale by breaking up its outline. This makes it hard to see as it flits through the water.

SURPRISE!
Orcas are one of the few whales that come onto shore, on purpose (pp. 56–57). On the Peninsula Valdes in Argentina and the Crozet Islands in the Indian Ocean, orcas swim up onto the beach to grab baby sea lions. Then they use their front flippers to turn around and wiggle back into the surf, the sea lion held firmly in their jaws.

LIKE A CAT WITH A MOUSE
All is not yet over for the sea lion. The orca plays with the limp animal like a cat with a mouse. It will fling its prey high into the air with a quick flick of the tail. Young orcas have to learn how to do this, and often join their parents in the game. Finally the terrified sea lion is eaten.

PEA IN A POD
This female killer
is only seven years old and already weighs two tonnes.
Both males and females remain in the same pod as their
mother for life. An older female seems to be in charge of
the pod. Orcas never mate within a pod, but only when
two pods meet. They breach and lobtail a lot during
these exciting encounters.

IT'S A FAMILY AFFAIR
This orca pod lives in British Columbia, Canada. They belong to
the best studied population of whales anywhere in the world.
The 200 plus individuals are easily recognized by the nicks in
their dorsal fins (p. 60) and the shapes of their "saddles", the
grey patches behind the fins. The mature male in this pod has a
huge dorsal fin. These can grow to be 2 m (6 ft) tall.

SHOULD I STAY OR SHOULD I GO?
Orcas live in every ocean of the world. Researchers in
British Columbia have found two types. Resident
orcas stay in one area, where they eat fish
and squid and make a lot of underwater
sounds. In contrast, transients
(wanderers) roam widely. They
move stealthily and silently
and tackle larger prey
like seals and other
whales.

Melon

Blow-hole

BIG SUCKERS
Fishermen and orcas are often in
conflict. In many areas, the fishermen feel that orcas eat valuable
salmon and herring. The whales
are clever. In Alaska, orcas follow
fishing boats and gently suck the
fish from the lines as they are
hauled in. All the fishermen
pull up are the fishes' lips.

The amazing narwhal

THE MYTHICAL UNICORN, a white horse with a horn growing out of its forehead, was really a whale – the "unicorn-whale" or narwhal. Narwhal tusks were on sale in Europe long before the real animal was widely known, so it was easy for imaginative traders to claim that the tusks came from unicorns. Even today the narwhal is a mysterious animal. We are still not certain what its strange overgrown tooth is for, though there are many ideas. Like its close relative the beluga, the narwhal lives in the remote, icy waters of the Arctic, where it is hard to study. Both narwhals and belugas migrate with the seasons, following the receding ice north in the summer and south in the winter. As the sea freezes over, they are sometimes trapped in the ice. They can usually keep breathing holes open, but many narwhals and belugas probably drown when the ice catches them far from open water.

THE UNICORN
In the Middle Ages, narwhal tusks were sold as unicorn horns, which were thought to have magical properties. Cups made from them were supposed to neutralize any poison. The tusks were also ground into a medicinal powder. This was still on sale in Japan in the 1950s under the name of *ikkaku*.

Fan-shaped tail, more marked in older narwhals

Row of low bumps instead of dorsal fin

Right tooth, which usually does not grow beyond the gums

Pectoral flipper

Left tooth or tusk grows in an anti-clockwise spiral

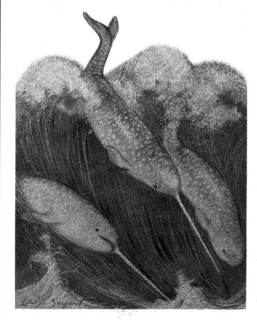

WHAT'S IT FOR?
People have suggested all kinds of uses for the narwhal's tusk. Some guess that the giant tooth is used to spear fish or to break holes in the ice. Others say the narwhal may use it as a hoe to root out animals on the ocean floor. But all these ideas are probably wrong, because they do not explain why males have tusks, while females survive very well without them!

LONG IN THE TOOTH
A bottom view of a male narwhal's skull shows the roots of its mighty tooth. All narwhals have two teeth, though in females they almost never grow beyond the gums. The same is usually true for a male's right tooth, while the left grows out to become the tusk. In adults, the tusk can be 3 m (10 ft), more than half as long as the whale's body. Every now and then a female grows a tusk, or a male grows two. Two-tusked skulls were especially prized, and there are quite a few of them in museums.

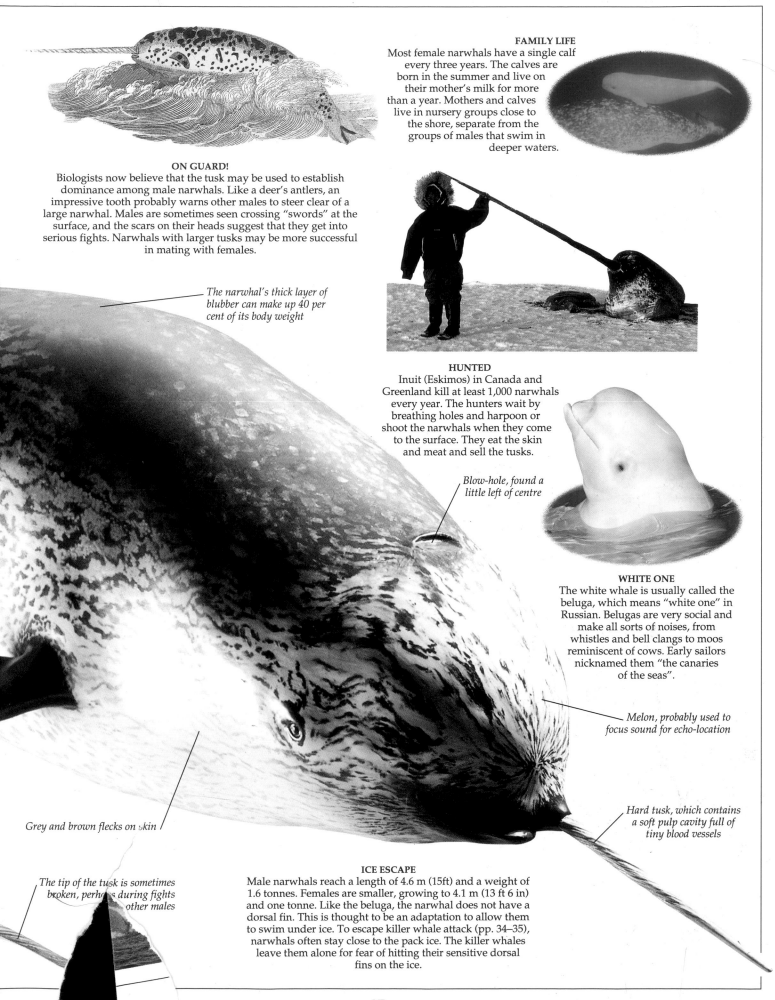

ON GUARD!

Biologists now believe that the tusk may be used to establish dominance among male narwhals. Like a deer's antlers, an impressive tooth probably warns other males to steer clear of a large narwhal. Males are sometimes seen crossing "swords" at the surface, and the scars on their heads suggest that they get into serious fights. Narwhals with larger tusks may be more successful in mating with females.

FAMILY LIFE

Most female narwhals have a single calf every three years. The calves are born in the summer and live on their mother's milk for more than a year. Mothers and calves live in nursery groups close to the shore, separate from the groups of males that swim in deeper waters.

The narwhal's thick layer of blubber can make up 40 per cent of its body weight

HUNTED

Inuit (Eskimos) in Canada and Greenland kill at least 1,000 narwhals every year. The hunters wait by breathing holes and harpoon or shoot the narwhals when they come to the surface. They eat the skin and meat and sell the tusks.

Blow-hole, found a little left of centre

WHITE ONE

The white whale is usually called the beluga, which means "white one" in Russian. Belugas are very social and make all sorts of noises, from whistles and bell clangs to moos reminiscent of cows. Early sailors nicknamed them "the canaries of the seas".

Melon, probably used to focus sound for echo-location

Hard tusk, which contains a soft pulp cavity full of tiny blood vessels

Grey and brown flecks on skin

The tip of the tusk is sometimes broken, perhaps during fights with other males

ICE ESCAPE

Male narwhals reach a length of 4.6 m (15ft) and a weight of 1.6 tonnes. Females are smaller, growing to 4.1 m (13 ft 6 in) and one tonne. Like the beluga, the narwhal does not have a dorsal fin. This is thought to be an adaptation to allow them to swim under ice. To escape killer whale attack (pp. 34–35), narwhals often stay close to the pack ice. The killer whales leave them alone for fear of hitting their sensitive dorsal fins on the ice.

The sperm whale

Sperm whale rib

SPERM WHALES HAVE THE LARGEST brains that have ever existed and a family life that spans the globe. They are creatures of the open ocean that dive to incredible depths to feed on squid, a food resource that is out of reach of most other predators. A male sperm whale eats more than a tonne of squid a day, and every year sperm whales eat more food than the total amount caught by all the world's fishermen. We still know little about how the whale hunts in its dark underwater world. The function of its huge square forehead is also unclear. It may help the sperm whale dive to such amazing depths. The whale may even use its head to produce powerful clicks to stun its prey.

THE WHITE WHALE
The most famous sperm whale is Moby Dick, the hero of Herman Melville's novel. It is the story of Captain Ahab, who has lost a leg in a battle with the huge white whale. He becomes obsessed with killing the whale and hunts it all over the globe. In the end, Moby Dick sinks the ship and the captain goes down with it. Albino (white) sperm whales do occur, but they are very rare.

MADEIRA SPERM WHALE
Catching sperm whales from open boats was a dangerous occupation (pp. 46–47). Until a few years ago, whales were still killed in this way off Madeira and the Azores Islands in the Atlantic Ocean. The Azores population is still healthy, but there are few sperm whales left off Madeira.

Nicks on the trailing edge of tail flukes are used by researchers to identify individuals

PYGMY SPERM
Almost nothing is known about the pygmy and dwarf sperm whales, the other members of the family. Both are relatively small, less than 3 m (10 ft) long. Like the sperm whale, they are deep divers that live in the open ocean.

FOUL-SMELLING PEARL
Once worth its weight in gold, ambergris is a foul-smelling wax that was used to make perfumes. It is occasionally secreted in the sperm whale's guts, perhaps around squid beaks. For whalers, finding a lump of ambergris was a valuable prize. It sometimes washes ashore in places like the Maldive Islands, to the delight of the local people.

GIANT SQUID
Only one man, a whaler by the name of Frank Bullen, has ever seen a battle between a giant squid and a sperm whale. The largest squid ever found in a whale's stomach was 12 m (39 ft) long! But the average size is much smaller, and even monster squid must have little chance against a sperm whale. The famous "battles" are probably just the squid wriggling to try and get out of the whale's jaws.

MAKING A SPLASH
This sperm whale is lobtailing – lifting its muscular tail flukes into the air and slamming them down on the water. Like breaching (p. 27), this is probably a way of communicating. It is usually females that lobtail, often in the presence of males. The big splashes made by lobtailing and breaching can be heard under water a long way off.

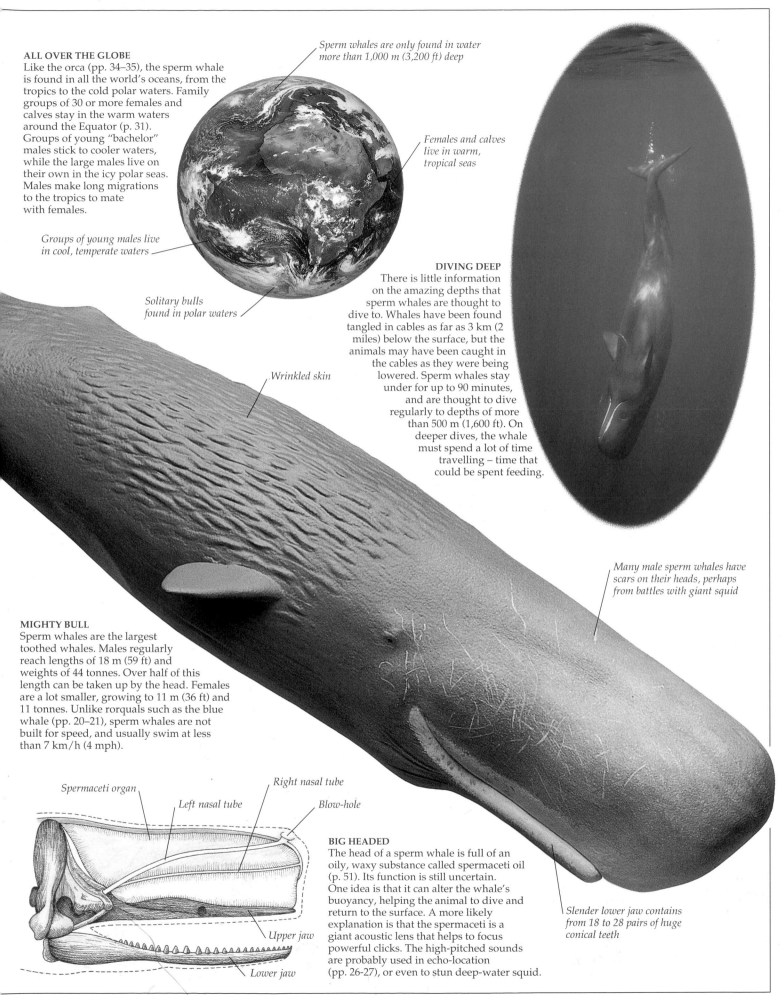

ALL OVER THE GLOBE

Like the orca (pp. 34–35), the sperm whale is found in all the world's oceans, from the tropics to the cold polar waters. Family groups of 30 or more females and calves stay in the warm waters around the Equator (p. 31). Groups of young "bachelor" males stick to cooler waters, while the large males live on their own in the icy polar seas. Males make long migrations to the tropics to mate with females.

Sperm whales are only found in water more than 1,000 m (3,200 ft) deep

Females and calves live in warm, tropical seas

Groups of young males live in cool, temperate waters

Solitary bulls found in polar waters

Wrinkled skin

DIVING DEEP

There is little information on the amazing depths that sperm whales are thought to dive to. Whales have been found tangled in cables as far as 3 km (2 miles) below the surface, but the animals may have been caught in the cables as they were being lowered. Sperm whales stay under for up to 90 minutes, and are thought to dive regularly to depths of more than 500 m (1,600 ft). On deeper dives, the whale must spend a lot of time travelling – time that could be spent feeding.

Many male sperm whales have scars on their heads, perhaps from battles with giant squid

MIGHTY BULL

Sperm whales are the largest toothed whales. Males regularly reach lengths of 18 m (59 ft) and weights of 44 tonnes. Over half of this length can be taken up by the head. Females are a lot smaller, growing to 11 m (36 ft) and 11 tonnes. Unlike rorquals such as the blue whale (pp. 20–21), sperm whales are not built for speed, and usually swim at less than 7 km/h (4 mph).

Spermaceti organ

Left nasal tube

Right nasal tube

Blow-hole

BIG HEADED

The head of a sperm whale is full of an oily, waxy substance called spermaceti oil (p. 51). Its function is still uncertain. One idea is that it can alter the whale's buoyancy, helping the animal to dive and return to the surface. A more likely explanation is that the spermaceti is a giant acoustic lens that helps to focus powerful clicks. The high-pitched sounds are probably used in echo-location (pp. 26-27), or even to stun deep-water squid.

Slender lower jaw contains from 18 to 28 pairs of huge conical teeth

Upper jaw

Lower jaw

The elephant seal

T HE ELEPHANT seal gets its name from the male's huge, swollen nose. He uses it in an incredible mating ritual. Elephant seals are enormous, up to three tonnes. They come ashore in large groups to mate, give birth, and suckle their young. There is constant activity on the crowded beaches as the biggest, strongest males battle for places among the females, while less dominant males hang around the edges. The pups and females grunt and groan and the males roar. These beaches are dangerous places for people, who could be attacked by an aggressive male. There are two species of elephant seal, southern and northern. Though they live thousands of kilometres apart, they are thought to be closely related. Northern elephant seals are found off the west coast of North America, where they haul out (come ashore) on isolated islands from San Francisco to Baja, Mexico. Southern elephant seals are found all around the Antarctic.

WHAT A SCHNOZZ!
Male elephants seals are up to ten times heavier than females (which do not have such large noses). Every male tries to control a harem (group) of females and keep other males away. He scares off rivals by bellowing, rearing up on his belly, and filling his nose with air. Hopefully that other males will think he is huge and leave him in peace.

NOSE JOB
Most animals just use their noses to smell. But the elephant's trunk is like an arm, good for picking up objects, even spraying water like a hose. The sperm whale has the largest nose of all. It probably uses this to focus sounds (p. 38–39).

BATTLE OF THE GIANTS
These two males are fighting for control of a beach crowded with females. These battles start with a lot of huffing and puffing and showing off of noses. Usually the smaller male then sneaks away and avoids a fight. But two big males may have a violent showdown. Most large males are covered in scars and bitemarks.

The elephant seal is a true seal, and cannot tuck its hind flippers under its body

BLUBBERING ABOUT
Elephant seals are deep divers. They are known to reach depths of over a kilometre below the surface (p. 61). At such depths the pressure is enormous. A fur coat would not keep the animal warm, because the bubbles trapped between the hairs would be compressed to almost nothing (p. 16). Instead elephant seals stay warm with thick layers of blubber.

Cranium (brain case)

Processes where strong neck muscles attach to spine

Neck vertebrae, not fused like a whale's

Massive lower jaw

Thoracic (chest) vertebrae

Tall processes, where swimming muscles attach to spine

Clavicle (collar bone)

Scapula (shoulder blade)

Lumbar (lower back) vertebrae

Humerus

Fibia

Pelvic girdle (hips)

Sternum

Ribs

Tibia

Phalanges (finger bones)

BARE BONES OF AN ELEPHANT SEAL
A seal's skeleton is more like a dog's than a whale's (pp. 12–13). The legs are modified into strong flippers, with long, strong "finger" bones. On land an elephant seal cannot lift its whole weight with its flippers, but keeps its belly on the ground and moves by flexing its back.

Femur

Wrist bones

Phalanges (toe bones)

TRUE LOVE?

The female elephant seal (on the left) cannot really say no when it comes to mating. The huge male pins her down and may bite her neck to keep her still. As soon as he finishes, he moves on to the next female.

MILK LIKE MAYONNAISE

Seal milk looks like mayonnaise. Southern elephant seal milk contains up to 43 per cent fat. The mother does not eat at all for the whole three to four weeks of suckling. She loses a lot of weight, while the pup puts it on fast. Some northern elephant seal pups grow even faster by sneaking milk from several females.

Half of body weight may be blubber

Large front flippers, used to steer while swimming

POLLUTED BEACH

A big threat to elephant seals these days is pollution. Most of this ugly rubbish is harmless. But seals often get tangled in packing straps and nets. As the seal grows, its neck or flipper is cut by the hard plastic. This is a slow and painful way to die.

WE ARE FAMILY

The northern elephant seal was hunted almost to extinction at the end of the 19th century (pp. 52–53). When the killing stopped, there were less than a hundred seals left. This small band of survivors made an incredible recovery, and all the animals alive today are descended from them. The population has reached 120,000. But all these seals are closely related, and people are worried that they may suffer from inbreeding.

Hind flippers, the seal's driving force

I am the walrus

WITH ITS HUGE TUSKS, bushy moustache, and thick rolls of blubber, the walrus is unlike any other seal. For this reason it is put in a family all its own. There are about 250,000 walruses left, all found in the cold waters of the North Pacific and Atlantic oceans. They live in large groups which huddle together for warmth. The life cycle of the walrus follows the seasonal ebb and flow of the Arctic ice. Females give birth in spring. Then they migrate as far as 3,000 km (1,800 miles) north following the melting ice. Despite their huge size, walruses have two formidable enemies, polar bears (p. 7) and killer whales. In the Canadian Arctic, bears are often seen chasing or sneaking up on walruses. In Russia, polar bears have even been seen throwing chunks of ice at them! A pod of killer whales (pp. 34–35) will hunt together, rounding up the walruses and taking it in turns to swim through the middle of the herd with their jaws open wide. They may also ram ice floes to try and tip walruses into the sea.

TRADITIONAL FOOD SOURCE
The Inuit still kill walruses, as they always have. But in the last three centuries, Europeans hunted large numbers commercially (pp. 52–53). The herds suffered greatly, and only the North Pacific population has completely recovered.

TOOTH WALK
The German artist Albrecht Dürer drew a walrus pulling itself onto an ice floe with its tusks. This explains the Latin name, *Odobenus rosmarus*, which means "tooth-walking seahorse". Tusks are also useful for enlarging breathing holes in the ice.

THE TIME HAS COME, THE WALRUS SAID...
Lewis Carroll's famous story *Through the Looking-Glass* stars a walrus and a carpenter. They invite some oysters to take a walk with them. As you might have guessed, the oysters end up being eaten! In real life, walruses do eat shellfish, but they stick to bivalves like clams that live in the mud (p. 23). They spit jets of water into the murky sea floor to help root out their food.

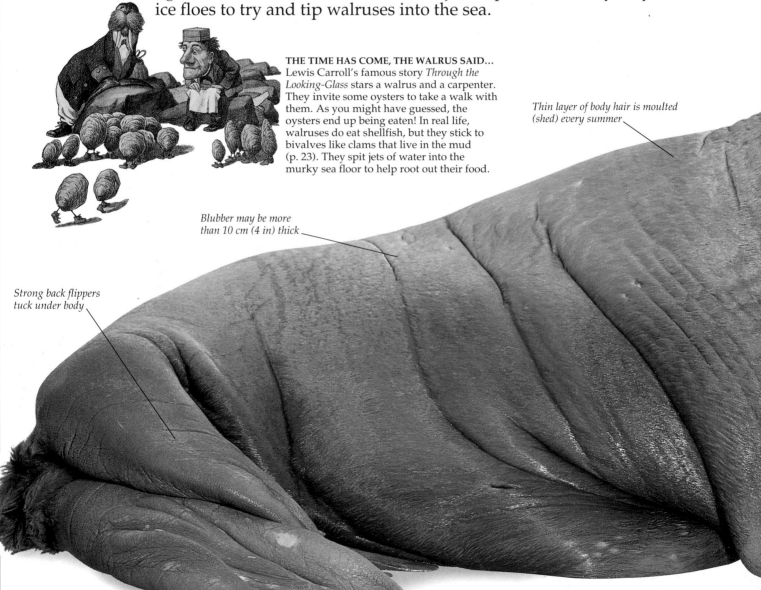

Thin layer of body hair is moulted (shed) every summer

Blubber may be more than 10 cm (4 in) thick

Strong back flippers tuck under body

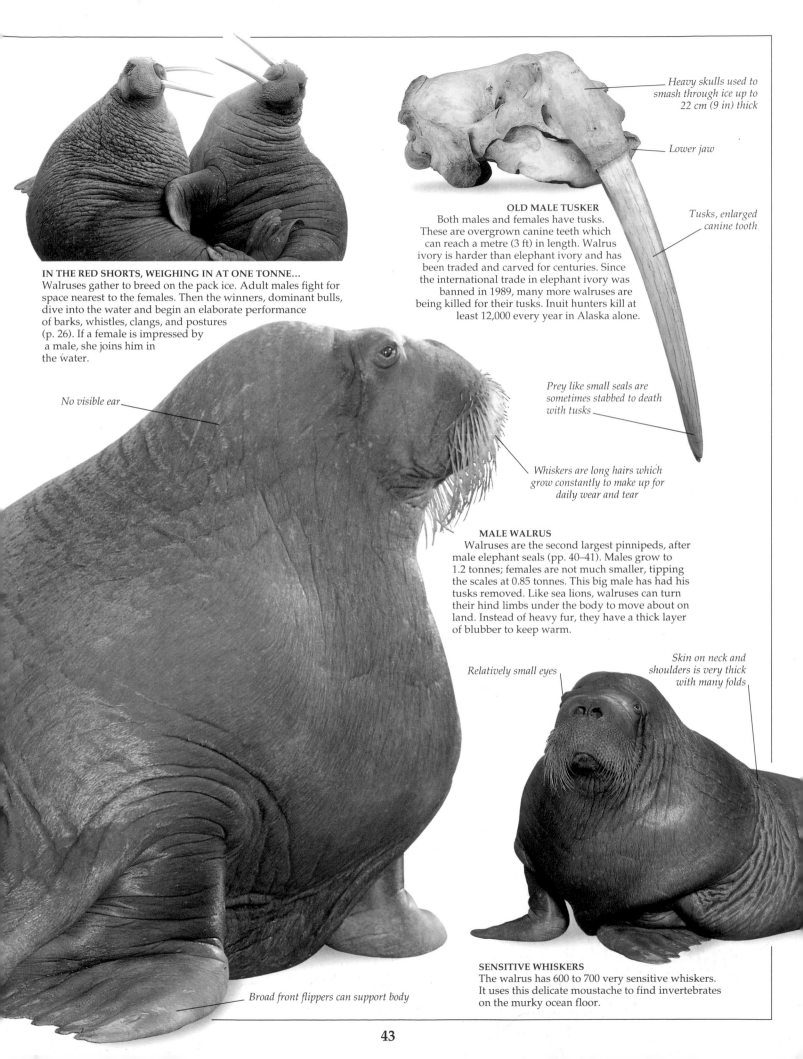

IN THE RED SHORTS, WEIGHING IN AT ONE TONNE...
Walruses gather to breed on the pack ice. Adult males fight for space nearest to the females. Then the winners, dominant bulls, dive into the water and begin an elaborate performance of barks, whistles, clangs, and postures (p. 26). If a female is impressed by a male, she joins him in the water.

Heavy skulls used to smash through ice up to 22 cm (9 in) thick

Lower jaw

OLD MALE TUSKER
Both males and females have tusks. These are overgrown canine teeth which can reach a metre (3 ft) in length. Walrus ivory is harder than elephant ivory and has been traded and carved for centuries. Since the international trade in elephant ivory was banned in 1989, many more walruses are being killed for their tusks. Inuit hunters kill at least 12,000 every year in Alaska alone.

Tusks, enlarged canine tooth

Prey like small seals are sometimes stabbed to death with tusks

No visible ear

Whiskers are long hairs which grow constantly to make up for daily wear and tear

MALE WALRUS
Walruses are the second largest pinnipeds, after male elephant seals (pp. 40–41). Males grow to 1.2 tonnes; females are not much smaller, tipping the scales at 0.85 tonnes. This big male has had his tusks removed. Like sea lions, walruses can turn their hind limbs under the body to move about on land. Instead of heavy fur, they have a thick layer of blubber to keep warm.

Relatively small eyes

Skin on neck and shoulders is very thick with many folds

Broad front flippers can support body

SENSITIVE WHISKERS
The walrus has 600 to 700 very sensitive whiskers. It uses this delicate moustache to find invertebrates on the murky ocean floor.

Sea cows

MERMAID
Since ancient times, sailors have told stories of mermaids, beautiful women with fishes' tails. The legends are probably based on sightings of dugongs or manatees. But you would have to spend a long time at sea to imagine a dugong was a beautiful woman! Mermaids were bad omens and were said to lure ships onto rocks.

WITH THEIR FLESHY SNOUTS, chubby bodies, and gentle ways, it is not surprising that manatees and dugongs are often called sea cows. The three species of manatee and the single species of dugong all live in warm waters. They are slow-moving vegetarians, grazing on sea grass, water hyacinths, and occasionally seaweed. Manatees all stay in rivers or salty estuaries and rarely venture into the open sea. This makes the dugong the only vegetarian marine mammal.

Like whales, manatees and dugongs have lost their back legs and spend their entire lives in the water. Also like whales, they reproduce slowly, giving birth to a single calf every three years. This makes them very vulnerable to extinction. Wherever they occur, dugongs are hunted for their tasty meat. Many manatees and dugongs are also killed in collisions with boats.

West Indian manatee

Brazilian manatee

African manatee

Dugong

WHERE THEY LIVE
Of the three species of manatee, one never leaves the Amazon River, while the other two live in estuaries as well as rivers. The dugong is entirely marine (sea-going).

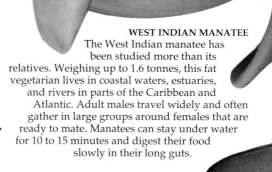

WEST INDIAN MANATEE
The West Indian manatee has been studied more than its relatives. Weighing up to 1.6 tonnes, this fat vegetarian lives in coastal waters, estuaries, and rivers in parts of the Caribbean and Atlantic. Adult males travel widely and often gather in large groups around females that are ready to mate. Manatees can stay under water for 10 to 15 minutes and digest their food slowly in their long guts.

NOISY EATERS
Manatees and dugongs are specialized eaters, the only mammals that feed on underwater vegetation. Manatees are noisy eaters. When they feed at the surface, the chomping of their teeth and flapping of their lips are easy to hear. Semi-captive manatees have even been used as underwater lawn mowers, to clear waterways and dams choked with water hyacinths. In the sea, they eat varieties of sea grass.

POWER HUNGRY
This manatee has algae growing all over its back. If manatees get too cold, they become constipated and die. So in winter, they seek out warm waters such as hot springs. In Florida, manatees gather around the warm water outlets of power stations and factories. This may not be very good for their long-term health.

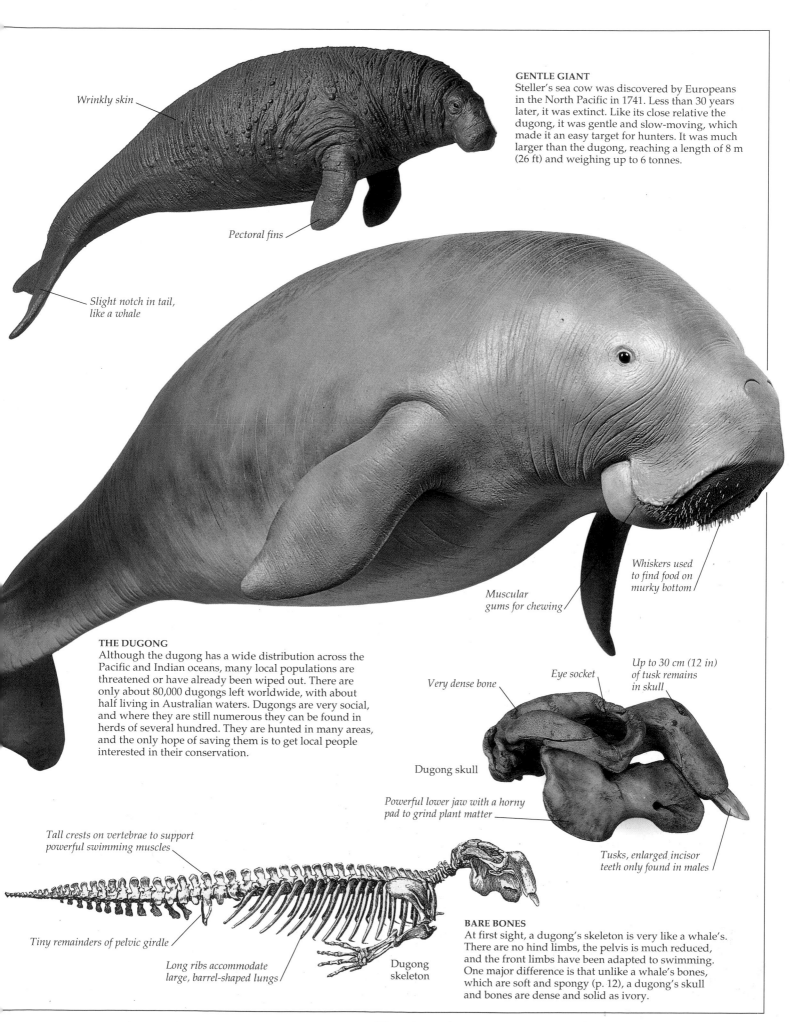

Wrinkly skin

GENTLE GIANT
Steller's sea cow was discovered by Europeans in the North Pacific in 1741. Less than 30 years later, it was extinct. Like its close relative the dugong, it was gentle and slow-moving, which made it an easy target for hunters. It was much larger than the dugong, reaching a length of 8 m (26 ft) and weighing up to 6 tonnes.

Pectoral fins

Slight notch in tail, like a whale

Whiskers used to find food on murky bottom

Muscular gums for chewing

THE DUGONG
Although the dugong has a wide distribution across the Pacific and Indian oceans, many local populations are threatened or have already been wiped out. There are only about 80,000 dugongs left worldwide, with about half living in Australian waters. Dugongs are very social, and where they are still numerous they can be found in herds of several hundred. They are hunted in many areas, and the only hope of saving them is to get local people interested in their conservation.

Very dense bone

Eye socket

Up to 30 cm (12 in) of tusk remains in skull

Dugong skull

Powerful lower jaw with a horny pad to grind plant matter

Tusks, enlarged incisor teeth only found in males

Tall crests on vertebrae to support powerful swimming muscles

Tiny remainders of pelvic girdle

Long ribs accommodate large, barrel-shaped lungs

Dugong skeleton

BARE BONES
At first sight, a dugong's skeleton is very like a whale's. There are no hind limbs, the pelvis is much reduced, and the front limbs have been adapted to swimming. One major difference is that unlike a whale's bones, which are soft and spongy (p. 12), a dugong's skull and bones are dense and solid as ivory.

Hunting the mighty whale

PEOPLE HAVE HUNTED WHALES for two thousand years. For early whalers like the Vikings, the whale was a sea monster to be conquered in a desperate battle. In the last century, whaling was a dangerous occupation. Ships set sail for the frozen and uncharted Arctic. When a whale was seen, tiny boats were lowered and rowed silently up to the unsuspecting giant. Hand harpoons were thrown into the whale. In the struggle, boats were often overturned and men drowned. Even in those early days, far too many whales were killed and the whalers had to move from place to place to find new stocks (populations) to hunt. Soon large Yankee (American) ships were sailing the world in search of whales.

YANKEE WHALING BOAT
When the lookout saw a whale spouting, he let out the traditional cry "Thar she blows!" Then boats were lowered and the whale was harpooned. This model of a Yankee whaling boat is made from sperm whale bones. In the Arctic, the whale was towed ashore to be cut up and boiled down for its oil. But sperm whales are creatures of the open ocean (pp. 38–39), and Yankee whalers had to process them aboard ship.

WHALE OF A POT
Blubber pots were mounted in pairs on the ship's deck. They were filled with blubber and a fire was lit below to extract the oil. This was ladled off, cooled, and poured into storage casks.

KEEPING A GRIP
Keeping your footing on a whale's slippery back was no easy task. So the whalers who flensed (cut up) the whale wore sharp spurs on their boots, like the crampons used by mountaineers.

A WHALER'S TOOLS
Whalers took a variety of tools on their long voyages. Harpoons were thrown from a distance. They were attached to a coil of rope which played out as the whale dived. When the injured, exhausted whale came up for the last time, it was killed with a lance from close quarters. The dead whale was then cut up with various flensing tools.

BENT IN BATTLE
Harpoons were made of soft iron, so they could be straightened if they were bent by the whale.

Bowsprit

Lance, used to kill whale

Dolphin striker, which holds down bowsprit

Blubber knife, for cutting through thick layers of fat

Flensing spade, for peeling back rolls of blubber

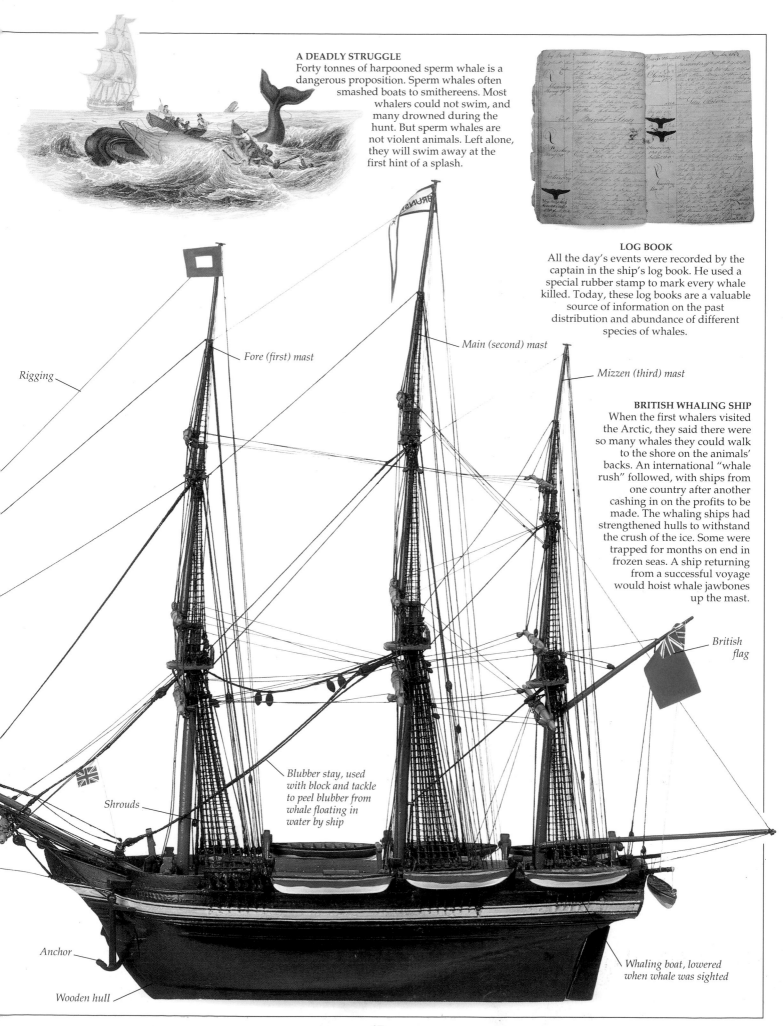

A DEADLY STRUGGLE
Forty tonnes of harpooned sperm whale is a dangerous proposition. Sperm whales often smashed boats to smithereens. Most whalers could not swim, and many drowned during the hunt. But sperm whales are not violent animals. Left alone, they will swim away at the first hint of a splash.

LOG BOOK
All the day's events were recorded by the captain in the ship's log book. He used a special rubber stamp to mark every whale killed. Today, these log books are a valuable source of information on the past distribution and abundance of different species of whales.

BRITISH WHALING SHIP
When the first whalers visited the Arctic, they said there were so many whales they could walk to the shore on the animals' backs. An international "whale rush" followed, with ships from one country after another cashing in on the profits to be made. The whaling ships had strengthened hulls to withstand the crush of the ice. Some were trapped for months on end in frozen seas. A ship returning from a successful voyage would hoist whale jawbones up the mast.

Fore (first) mast

Main (second) mast

Mizzen (third) mast

Rigging

British flag

Blubber stay, used with block and tackle to peel blubber from whale floating in water by ship

Shrouds

Anchor

Wooden hull

Whaling boat, lowered when whale was sighted

Whaling in the 20th century

STEAM-POWERED SHIPS and explosive harpoons revolutionized whaling. With these advances, whalers could hunt the fast rorquals like fin whales and the mighty blue (pp. 20–21). No animal was safe. The whalers travelled the world, slaughtering population after population. By the turn of the century, they had arrived in the remote, inhospitable waters of the Antarctic. At first the whalers towed dead whales back to shore stations on islands like South Georgia. Then factory ships that could process dead whales at sea one after another were built . In 1988, a worldwide moratorium (ban) finally brought a pause in commercial whaling. By then, the whalers were under a lot of pressure from conservationists. But the main reason most countries stopped was economic – there were not enough whales left!

WHAT A FLUKE!
A whaler is dwarfed by a sperm whale's tail fluke. Since 1946, whaling has been regulated by the International Whaling Commission (IWC). This began as a whaler's club that tried to control the price of whale oil. But now the IWC is looking very carefully at ways to protect the future of whales. It banned the commercial whaling of sperm whales after 1984.

HITTING THE WHALE
It is virtually impossible to kill a whale humanely. The vital organs are hard to hit from a moving vessel. Often the harpoons do not explode. Most whales are killed within a few minutes, but some struggle in agony for more than half an hour.

Tip loaded with grenade which explodes inside whale

Barbs open on impact so harpoon is embedded in flesh

FLENSING A BLUE
Before whaling started in the Antarctic, there were about 250,000 blue whales there. Now there may only be a few hundred left. This dead giant was 27.4 m (90 ft) long. The next species to be hunted was the smaller fin whale. Once they became hard to find, the whalers moved on to even smaller sei whales.

HARPOONING DOLPHINS
This whaler is harpooning dolphins that have come to bow ride on his boat (p. 32). Even today, there are few restrictions on the hunting of small whales, which are not covered by the IWC. In many countries, dolphins and porpoises are killed for food, sport, or even crab bait.

THE BOWHEAD HUNT
The Inuit have hunted small numbers of bowhead whales for many centuries. But because of European whaling, the bowhead is now on the verge of extinction (p. 63). These Inuit whalers are flensing (cutting up) a dead whale. They still kill a few bowheads every year. This is not considered a commercial hunt, because no part of the whale is sold.

THAR SHE BLEEDS
Until very recently, sperm whales were caught off the Atlantic islands of the Azores and Madeira (p. 38). The whalers used small *canoas* (sailing canoes) and hand harpoons, like the Yankee whalers of last century. They towed the dead whales back to stations on shore to be processed. Every year, the Azoreans managed to catch several hundred sperm whales with these primitive methods.

Calibrated sight

Muzzle

Trigger

Cradle which holds muzzle and pivots

MUZZLE-LOADING HARPOON GUN
Norwegian technology and expertise were important in developing the whaling industry all over the world. The Norwegians set up whaling operations in many countries, including Japan. This harpoon gun was made in Norway in 1925. It was used in Antarctic whaling. The gun was mounted on the bow of a boat and loaded with a harpoon with an explosive tip. It was solidly made to absorb the recoil, and accurately balanced so it was easy to aim.

FACTORY SHIP
This dead minke whale is being dragged into a Japanese factory ship. It will be cut up and processed on board. The countries that want to continue whaling have focused on minke whales, which reach a top length of 10 m (33 ft). In the past, this was too small to bother with. There are still a fair few minkes in the southern oceans, but whaling in the north may have reduced some populations by over half.

Oils, brushes, and corsets

THE EARLY WHALERS SUFFERED incredible hardships so the world could have brushes, oil, soap, candles, umbrellas, and corsets. In an age before petroleum or plastics, whales provided valuable raw materials for thousands of everyday objects. Right whales were killed for their oil and baleen (pp. 24–25). The oil was refined and sold to be burnt in lamps. Baleen, often given the misleading name "whalebone", was a tough, springy material used to stiffen corsets and as bristles for brushes. Sperm whales were hunted for the oil in their heads. At first this was burnt in lamps and used to make candles. As the machine age unfolded, sperm oil became a high-grade lubricant for motors and cars. The whaling of other species ended because there were not enough whales left. But sperm whaling ended with the discovery of petroleum, a cheaper source of oil. Nowadays, alternatives have been found for all whale products. But whale meat has become a gourmet food item in Japan, where it can sell for $160 a kilo.

TIGHT FIT
Women wore very uncomfortable clothes years ago. They were squeezed into elaborate corsets stiffened with baleen ("whalebone").

Necklace made from whale bone

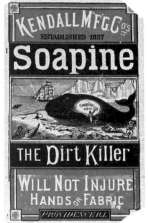

PILLS AND SOAP
Like all oils, whale oil can be turned into soap through a simple chemical process. Early in the 20th century, foods such as margarine and ice cream were also made from whale oil.

SCRAPING A LIVING
Many whale-related industries were set up in whaling ports. Here baleen from right whales is being scraped clean before being manufactured into the various products on these pages. Two whaling ships can be seen in the port in the background.

Chimney sweep's brush with baleen bristles

Floor brush with baleen bristles

Comb made from baleen

BALEEN BRUSHES
These days most brushes are made from plastics. But a hundred years ago, baleen was shredded to make brush bristles.

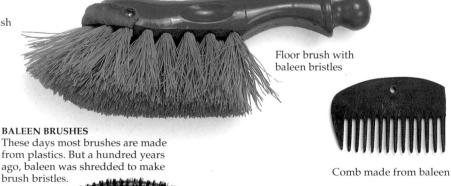

Hair brush with baleen bristles

50

SCRIMSHAW
On their long voyages, whalers passed the time decorating whales' teeth and bones. This is called scrimshaw. The designs were made more visible by rubbing soot into the scratches.

BURNING BRIGHT
What a live sperm whale does with the litres of oil in its huge head is still a mystery (pp. 38–39). Whalers had no problems finding a use for the oil. These spermaceti oil candles burn with a bright, clear flame. Engravings of Yankee whalers often show them bathed in the light of a thousand such lamps and candles.

SPERMACETI CANDLES from NANTUCKET ISLAND, MASS.

UMBRELLA
Old umbrellas had ribs made of springy baleen. Nowadays these have been replaced with steel or plastic.

Baleen ribs

GET YOUR WHALE MEAT!
With the advent of plastics and petroleum, the market for whale products almost disappeared. Now the main product is whale meat for eating. This Norwegian fishing boat has caught a whale to supplement its income. Some of the meat is sold locally on the quay, but most is exported to Japan.

ONE PAIR   DAWBARN'S   BLA-
Genuine WHITE WHALE Boot Laces
HAND-CUT   WALONGA BRAND   NO TAGS
MADE IN ENGLAND   MARKET HARBOROUGH, LEICESTERSHIRE
These Laces should not be pulled or jerked violently when first placed in the shoes

BELUGA BOOT LACES
These boot laces were made from the skin of belugas (white whales, p. 37). Whale oil was used to soften all kinds of leather.

Dyed baleen bristles ready to be made into brushes

Handle made from whale's bone

Whale meat extract   Whale meal   Whale liver oil   Sperm oil

RAW MATERIALS
Whale meat extract was used to manufacture margarine. Animal feed and pet food were made from whale meal. Whale liver oil was a source of vitamin A, and sperm oil was a machine lubricant.

Seal hunting

MOVING TARGET
The Inuit hunted seals from small sealskin boats called kayaks. The harpoon line was attached to a float, a seal bladder blown up like a balloon. If the harpooned seal put up a struggle, the hunter would throw the line and float overboard rather than risk capsizing the kayak.

LIKE WHALES, seals have been hunted for centuries. The story of sealing is not as well known, but it is just as bloody. The Inuit (Eskimo) people of the Arctic have always hunted seals. They made use of every bit of the seal, eating its meat, making clothes and boats from its skin, and burning seal oil in lamps. They never killed a lot of seals. But in the last two centuries, reckless commercial hunting did great damage to many seal populations. In the southern oceans, millions of elephant and fur seals were killed.

Huge numbers of walruses died in the Arctic, and the northern elephant seal was brought within a whisker of extinction (p. 41). But unlike whales, many seal populations have recovered. Sealing continues today, but the market for seal products is small.

Flint spearhead

Bone harpoon

Shaft carved from a whale penis bone

Inuit stone sculpture of seal hunter, from northern Canada

Head carved from seal bone

Wooden paw

ICE SCRATCHER
Another way of catching seals is to build a small shelter on the ice right next to a breathing hole. The Inuit hunter would stand by the hole for hours on end, a harpoon raised ready to strike. To stop his feet from freezing, he stood on a folded sealskin. The first sign of a seal would be the sound of its breathing. This scratcher from Alaska was rubbed on the ice to attract curious seals to the surface.

Soapstone

Bone knife

Seal breathing hole

Hunter dragging dead seal

SEALING SCENE
This seal hunting scene was etched onto a walrus tusk (pp. 42–43). The successful hunters are dragging dead seals with harpoon lines. Many Inuit myths are about seals. They believe that seals are always thirsty, so when one is killed, the hunter puts water to its lips.

Open sea *Hunter in kayak*

Wooden handle

HARPOON
Wood is scarce in the Arctic. This harpoon is made from driftwood, stone, and whale bones.

Figure of hunter

Harpoon thrower

MODEL HUNTER
This model of a man in a kayak shows the various harpoons and other implements of a seal hunter. Inuit men first made models like this for their children to play with. Later they gave them to European whalers and sealers in exchange for guns or metal tools.

Harpoon lashed to deck

WALRUS HUNT
As soon as Europeans arrived in Canada, they started killing seals. Huge numbers of walruses were shot from boats for their oil, tusks, and leather.

NASTY PICK
Seals have thin skulls. Sealers in the Arctic used picks like this to kill their prey with a quick blow to the head.

LAST MOMENTS
The killing of harp seals in Canada for their fur became an international controversy. Many people think the hunt is cruel and wasteful. The seals are clubbed on the head, and pups are often killed in front of their mothers. Hunters only take the fur and leave the body.

GRIZZLY TRADE
These sealers are hacking tusks out of walruses' heads. Walruses were the first seals to be hunted commercially, because they gather in huge herds. When there were almost none left, the sealers turned to grey seals. These are much smaller, but they still contain a lot of valuable oil.

WILD GRAFFITI
Conservation and animal welfare groups campaigned to end the harp seal hunt. This worker is spraying a pup with dye. This will make its fur worthless to hunters, who may spare it. Film of the seal hunt was shown on TV all over the world.

Purse made from seal fur

MONEY TALKS
Pressure from conservationists led the European Community to ban harp and hooded seal products. Many Canadians are very bitter about this. They claim that the seals are not endangered and should be killed because they eat valuable fish.

Harp seal pup

Myths and legends

THE BEAUTY AND MYSTERY of whales and seals have captured imaginations for centuries. Dolphins feature in the art and myths of most sea-faring nations, and there are many stories of dolphins saving drowning people or helping fishermen to catch fish. Some of these stories are true, and it is often hard to tell myth from fact. Killing dolphins is forbidden in many countries, and the ancient Greeks thought it was as bad as murdering a person. The people of the Amazon say that during fiestas, river dolphins come to shore dressed as men and woo pretty girls. In the Middle Ages, there were all sorts of legends surrounding the narwhal's amazing tusk (pp. 36–37). Strandings of whales are also mentioned in many medieval stories. The dead giants were seen as good or bad omens (p. 56).

GOLD KILLER
This gold killer whale box was carved by Bill Reid. He is part Haida, from the west coast of Canada. The Haida tell stories of the evil ocean people, who used killer whales as canoes. One day they turned a Haida chief into a killer whale. Now this whale protects the Haida from the attacks of the ocean people.

FLIPPER, KING OF THE SEA
The first whale to become a TV star was Flipper, a bottlenose dolphin. When people were in trouble and needed rescuing, Flipper was always there to save the day. Flipper's special friend was a young boy.

Silver coin from Greek colony of Syracuse, 480–479 B.C.

Roman coin from 2nd century B.C.

DOLPHIN COINS
There are many ancient Greek and Roman tales and legends about dolphins. One Roman story tells of a boy who was swimming along when a dolphin came up beneath him. The dolphin took him for a ride before pushing him back to the beach. Soon everyone in the village – even the grown-ups – were swimming and playing with the friendly dolphin.

Eros, the ancient Greek god of love

Dolphin

STARSTRUCK
This terracotta figure shows Eros, the Greek god of love, riding a dolphin. In one Greek myth, the god Orion is carried into the sky on the back of a dolphin. The gods gave him three stars, which became the constellation Orion's Belt,

NEPTUNE'S FRIEND
In this ancient Roman mosaic from a villa in North Africa, a dolphin is carrying Neptune's trident. Neptune was the god of the sea, the Roman version of the Greek god Poseidon. Here he is shown as part horse, part fish, and part man.

BOY AND DOLPHIN

Solitary dolphins around the world seem to seek out human company. They often develop special relationships with certain people and spend hours playing with them. Through history there are many stories of dolphins rescuing drowning people. Some of them are probably true.

Statue of boy and dolphin by English artist David Wynne (born 1926)

STOMACH FULL

In real life, Jonah could never have survived for three days in the belly of a whale (p. 12). There would be no air to breathe and he would suffocate in no time. There is a story of a 19th-century whaler who was swallowed by a sperm whale and found alive when the whale was killed several hours later. Could this incredible story be true?

SEAL STORIES

In many seal legends, the seal disguises itself as a person. In the Orkney Islands off the north coast of Scotland, they tell stories of "selchies". These seals come ashore and behave like people. One story tells of a hunter who married a beautiful girl he met on the beach. One day, she found her fur coat, which he had hidden after they met. She put it on, turned into a seal, and swam away. Tragically, her husband later killed her on a hunting trip.

GREEK SEA LION

This fanciful sea lion has the head of a lion, the hooves of a horse, and the tail of a dolphin.

OUT OF THE BIG BLUE

This is the poster for *The Big Blue*, a 1988 film by the French writer and director Luc Besson. It is the story of two divers, each trying to dive deeper than the other. One is cheery and sociable; the other gets on better with dolphins than people. With its superb underwater photography, *The Big Blue* made millions of people interested in dolphins.

Ancient Greek black figure jar with sea lion, 500–470 B.C.

Strandings and whale watching

UNTIL RECENTLY, most people only saw big whales dead on the beach. This is called stranding. A stranded whale always attracts a crowd. Usually the whale has died at sea and washed up on the shore. But every year, many live whales swim out of the water and strand themselves. Why they do this is still a mystery. Rescuers try to save the whales by covering them with wet towels. This keeps them cool and stops their sensitive skins from burning. When the tide comes in, the whales are helped to swim free. But often they head straight back to the beach and strand again. These days, many people head out to sea to watch live whales. This is a growing industry in many countries.

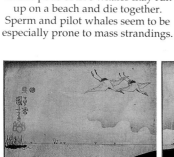

STRANDED PILOT
Whole pods of live whales may run up on a beach and die together. Sperm and pilot whales seem to be especially prone to mass strandings.

Huge baleen whale stranded on an English beach in 1924

The Stranded Whale, a woodblock print by the Japanese artist Kuniyoshi, about 1851

WHY DO THEY DO IT?
People have all sorts of explanations for live stranding. Some say that families strand together because one member of the group is ill. The whales may be lost or disorientated. But because we do not really know how they navigate, this is hard to prove. Strandings of dead whales may be caused by pollution (pp. 58–59), which weakens resistance to disease. Recent "die-offs" of dolphins in the Mediterranean and off the east coast of North America support this theory.

SAVED, LIVE ON TELEVISION
When winter approaches and the water begins to freeze, whales can become trapped by the advancing ice (pp. 36–37). In 1988, an international rescue was organized to save three gray whales trapped in the Arctic. Inuit workers kept the breathing hole open with chainsaws, while the whole world watched on television. Finally, Russian icebreaker ships cleared a safe path to the sea.

ROYAL FISHES
Since the 14th century, all whales stranded in Britain have officially belonged to the king or queen and are called "Fishes Royal". This pleased Elizabeth I, who was fond of whale meat. In recent years, all strandings where reported to the coast guard. Because of these laws, Britain has kept very good stranding records.

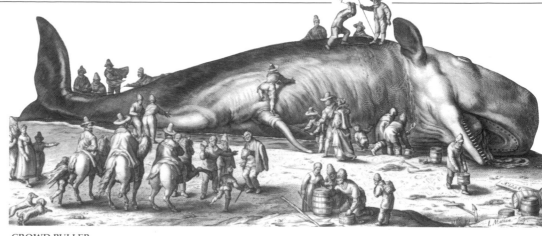

CROWD PULLER
On land, a dead whale's blubber insulates its body, so it warms up and decomposes fast. This is very smelly. The carcass becomes bloated with gases which make the whale more round. This huge sperm whale stranded on a Dutch beach in 1601. The local people thought it was an evil omen.

Watching whales
Around the world, there are many places to go whale watching. In some countries this is becoming a bigger industry than whaling ever was. In Japan and Norway, trips are led by ex-whalers. The gray whales in California are so friendly you can touch them from your canoe. In South Africa, it is forbidden to approach whales in boats, so people watch them from the shore. One town has a "whale crier" whose job is to let people know which bay the whales are in.

PERFORMING ANIMAL
Many people feel that dolphinaria are cruel circuses where the animals are trained to perform unnatural tricks. Their pools are tiny compared to the open ocean. It is very difficult to keep captive whales in good health, and many live short lives. For these reasons people in some countries have campaigned against dolphinaria. In Australia, the government has suggested that they be phased out.

CLOSE TO A KILLER
Dolphinaria are marine parks where people can come and see dolphins or killer whales. They provide the only chance for many people to see a whale. Our attitude to whales has changed partly because so many people have been able to enjoy them close up.

WHOAH!
Imagine watching a humpback leap right beside your boat. In some places whale watching is big business. Many boats provide spaces for scientists who can study the whales at the same time.

Fishing and pollution

NOW THAT MOST countries have stopped hunting them, the biggest threats whales and seals face are fishing and pollution. Every year, hundreds of thousands of whales and seals are drowned when they become tangled in fishing nets. The fishermen often view the mammals as pests. In countries like Norway and Canada, overfishing by people has reduced fish stocks. But the fishermen blame seals and whales for the problem and campaign for hunts to keep their numbers down (p. 53). The oceans are being used as a dustbin for the poisonous chemicals produced by industry. Once toxic chemicals have been released into the sea, it is impossible to recover them. They are invisible but deadly. Whales and seals are particularly at risk because many pollutants collect in their fat.

NO ACCIDENT
Seals and whales are usually tangled in nets by accident. But this Russian hunter has used a net to catch a rare Baikal seal (p. 63). He will sell the meat for food and the fur to make coats and hats.

INTO THE AIR AND SEA
Most methods of making paper produce highly poisonous chemicals. This is one of the paper mills that dump their waste into the world's largest freshwater lake, Lake Baikal in Russia. It is home to the endangered Baikal seal.

DOLPHIN TRAP
Trawlers catch fish by dragging nets like this one through the water. When two boats trawl together, the nets are so big that a whole school of dolphins could swim in and not be able to get out.

WHALE-SIZED MESS
Everyone is horrified when an oil tanker is wrecked and pours its oil into the sea. Clean-up teams can usually only recover a small part of the oil. It is much more important to prevent such disasters from happening in the first place.

SWIMMING IN OIL
When a sea otter (p. 7) gets covered in oil, its fur becomes matted. The animal has trouble keeping warm and may die of cold. In a desperate attempt to lick itself clean, the otter will also swallow poisonous oil. Hundreds of rare sea otters were hurt or killed in the *Exxon Valdez* oil spill in Alaska in 1989. Oil damages habitats and poisons food supplies. Oil poured into the Persian Gulf during the Gulf War of 1991 harmed the sea grass beds where dugongs feed. No one knows what the long-term effects of such huge spills will be.

INVISIBLE POISONS
Many poisonous chemicals are dumped into the sea. Some are pesticides such as DDT. These are passed up the food chain and concentrated in the bodies of predators like seals and whales. We now know that female whales pass these pollutants directly to their young through their milk.

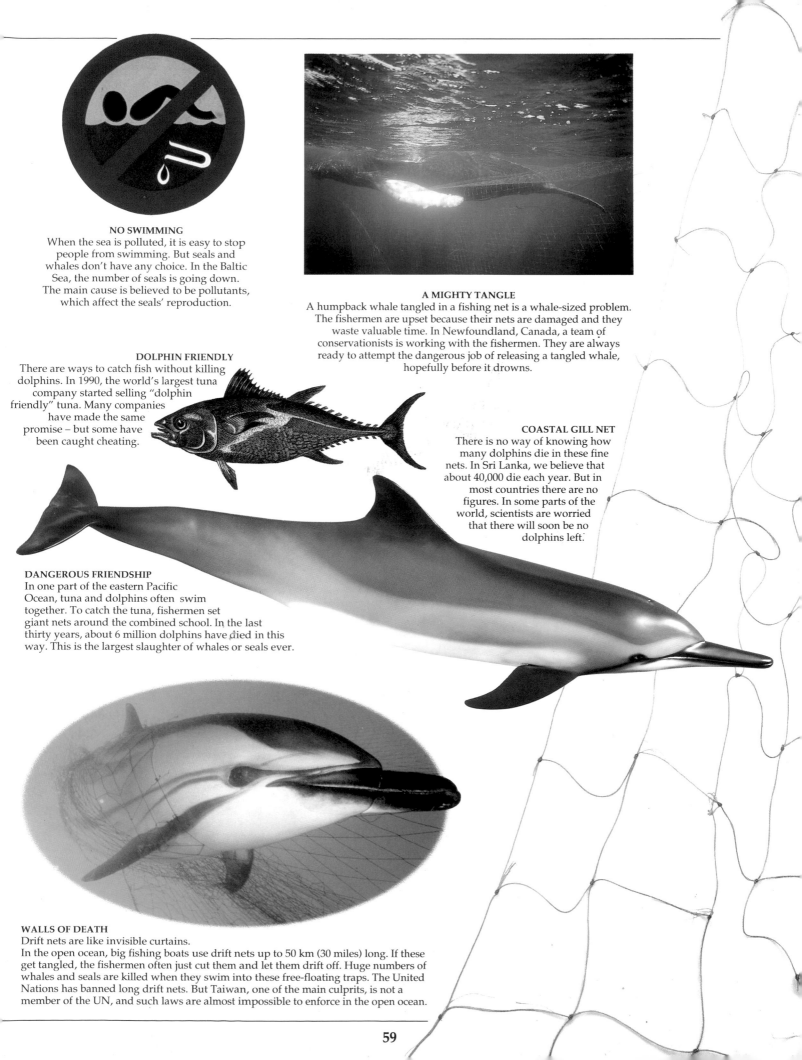

NO SWIMMING
When the sea is polluted, it is easy to stop people from swimming. But seals and whales don't have any choice. In the Baltic Sea, the number of seals is going down. The main cause is believed to be pollutants, which affect the seals' reproduction.

A MIGHTY TANGLE
A humpback whale tangled in a fishing net is a whale-sized problem. The fishermen are upset because their nets are damaged and they waste valuable time. In Newfoundland, Canada, a team of conservationists is working with the fishermen. They are always ready to attempt the dangerous job of releasing a tangled whale, hopefully before it drowns.

DOLPHIN FRIENDLY
There are ways to catch fish without killing dolphins. In 1990, the world's largest tuna company started selling "dolphin friendly" tuna. Many companies have made the same promise – but some have been caught cheating.

COASTAL GILL NET
There is no way of knowing how many dolphins die in these fine nets. In Sri Lanka, we believe that about 40,000 die each year. But in most countries there are no figures. In some parts of the world, scientists are worried that there will soon be no dolphins left.

DANGEROUS FRIENDSHIP
In one part of the eastern Pacific Ocean, tuna and dolphins often swim together. To catch the tuna, fishermen set giant nets around the combined school. In the last thirty years, about 6 million dolphins have died in this way. This is the largest slaughter of whales or seals ever.

WALLS OF DEATH
Drift nets are like invisible curtains.
In the open ocean, big fishing boats use drift nets up to 50 km (30 miles) long. If these get tangled, the fishermen often just cut them and let them drift off. Huge numbers of whales and seals are killed when they swim into these free-floating traps. The United Nations has banned long drift nets. But Taiwan, one of the main culprits, is not a member of the UN, and such laws are almost impossible to enforce in the open ocean.

Studying sea mammals

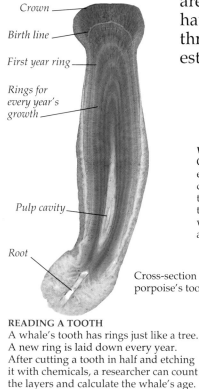

French engraving from 19th century showing scientists studying a model whale

WE STILL KNOW VERY LITTLE about the lives of seals and whales. The first information on anatomy came from cutting up dead animals, and the contents of the stomach or ovaries gave clues on diet or reproduction. More recently, many new techniques that do not harm animals have been developed. Some involve photography; others require small tissue samples. Whales live in a world of sound (pp. 26–27), and an underwater microphone can be used to find, follow, and even count them. One of the hardest questions to answer is: "How many whales are there?" Scientists and mathematicians have been working on this problem for three decades. But we still have only rough estimates for the size of most populations.

JACQUES COUSTEAU
This French adventurer has made many popular films and books about life under the sea.

DNA FINGERPRINTING
Scientists can now use a small piece of skin or muscle to identify an individual animal. They do this by examining the animal's DNA, its genetic material. The result, a DNA fingerprint, looks something like a bar code. Scientists can then use the bands to identify close relatives, for example an animal's parents or sisters.

WHALES ALIVE
One of the best way to study whales in their element is from small sailing boats (motor boats can make a lot of noise). Researchers take photos to identify individuals. Microphones left under the water follow the whales' vocalizations. The whales' social life can be pieced together from all this information.

Crown

Birth line

First year ring

Rings for every year's growth

Pulp cavity

Root

Cross-section of harbour porpoise's tooth

READING A TOOTH
A whale's tooth has rings just like a tree. A new ring is laid down every year. After cutting a tooth in half and etching it with chemicals, a researcher can count the layers and calculate the whale's age. The appearance of the layers also gives clues to how well fed or healthy the whale was from one year to the next.

Scratches from other dolphin's teeth

Nicks caused by parasites, fights, or collisions with boats

HERE'S MY I.D.
Every humpback whale has a unique black-and-white pattern on the underside of its tail. Thousands of humpbacks have been photographed and their patterns recorded. Every time a whale is sighted, its pattern is checked against the catalogue to see if it has been spotted before. This allows scientists to count populations, follow whales as they migrate, and learn who they spend their time with.

SCRATCHED AND SCARRED
Whales collect scratches and scars as they swim through life. These tell-tale marks can be used to identify individual animals. This is easier with old whales, like this 25-year-old bottlenose dolphin, which have more scars. The problem is that marks may change, which makes identification uncertain!

EARLY DISSECTION

Much of our early information on whales comes from the whaling industry. Early whalers and scientists recorded every conceivable piece of information on the gigantic corpses. Now most of the questions that remain can only be answered by studying live animals.

Radio antenna

Remnants of moulted fur

Used satellite tag with moulted fur

Sensor which shows how deep seal is diving and how fast it is swimming

ON THE PULSE
This acoustic transmitter broadcasts the heartbeat. This changes drastically when the animal goes for a deep dive.

SATELLITE TAG
When the animal surfaces, the data stored in this transmitter is beamed to a satellite and on to the lab.

VHF tag which sends out a radio signal

Acoustic tag

Tags for tracking

How do you follow a seal or a whale without getting wet? One way is to attach a tag to its body. This can then send back information on where the animal goes, how fast it swims, or how deep it dives. The most sophisticated tags send their signals to satellites. These tags are expensive, but their signals can be tracked anywhere in the world.

SEEING UNDER THE SEA
This computer-generated map shows the movements of a tagged elephant seal. One seal swam an incredible 2,650 km (1,640 miles) in 70 days. This seal is looking for food along the edge of the continental shelf. Every vertical white line is a dive.

Tip of Antarctic continent

Sea level

Path of seal

Sea bottom over continental shelf

Edge of continental shelf

FOLLOWING HIS NOSE
Attaching tags to seals or whales is not an easy job. This big male elephant seal (pp. 40–41) has a tag glued to his head. When he moults in the spring, the tag will fall off with his old fur. Other tags are shot into the skin of whales. But some people think this is cruel.

Deep ocean bottom

Save the whale!

FLAGSHIP
The whale has become a symbol for the whole conservation movement. This inflatable whale brought along to a demonstration is wearing the flags of every country of the world.

THE FUTURE OF WHALES and seals depends on people from all over the world getting together and co-operating. The seas are a common resource. How should they be used? Will it ever be possible to catch whales humanely and without hunting them to extinction? Can we develop whale tourism instead? Is keeping dolphins in captivity cruel (p. 57)? How can we control pollution and the use of fishing nets (pp. 58–59)? Even agreeing which species are endangered is difficult. Many countries have different views on all these questions – usually for their own reasons. Because whales migrate, they do not just belong to the countries that want to hunt them. The only way forward is by international co-operation, rational discussion, and good science. People are becoming more aware of the problems, but this is only the first step. Good intentions must be followed by real action and commitment. Only then can we safeguard the future of these magnificent animals.

STAMP DUTY
Developing countries are becoming aware of conservation problems. These stamps from Sri Lanka show some of the country's marine mammals.

Whale drawing by Liam Bleach, age 5

Blue whale drawn by Domoniqua Douglas, age 5

STARTING EARLY
The best way to change attitudes to whales and seals is to get children interested at an early age. These days most children know a lot about environmental issues. Often they have to teach their parents!

Distinctive short, rounded snout

Whale drawing by Giuseppe Paese, age 6

ABORIGINAL WHALING
With a leap from his wooden boat, a man drives a long bamboo pole into a whale. Only two villages in Indonesia still hunt whales in this way. Elsewhere in the world, a few whales are still caught in traditional ways in Tonga, Alaska, and Bequia in the Caribbean. Hundreds of narwhals and belugas are killed every year in Greenland (pp. 36–37).

MASS SLAUGHTER
In the Færoe Islands between Scotland and Iceland, whole pods of pilot whales are still hunted. The whales are driven ashore and killed. There has been an international outcry against the hunt, and the hunters have been portrayed as cruel. But because the complaints come from outside the islands, the Færoese have become more determined than ever to continue the yearly hunt.

Endangered species

A few species of whale and seal are close to disappearing forever. There are few blue whales left in the southern oceans (pp. 20–21). The areas they roam are so vast that they may not be able to find a mate! Gray whales were almost extinct by 1946. Now the California population has gone up to about 20,000.

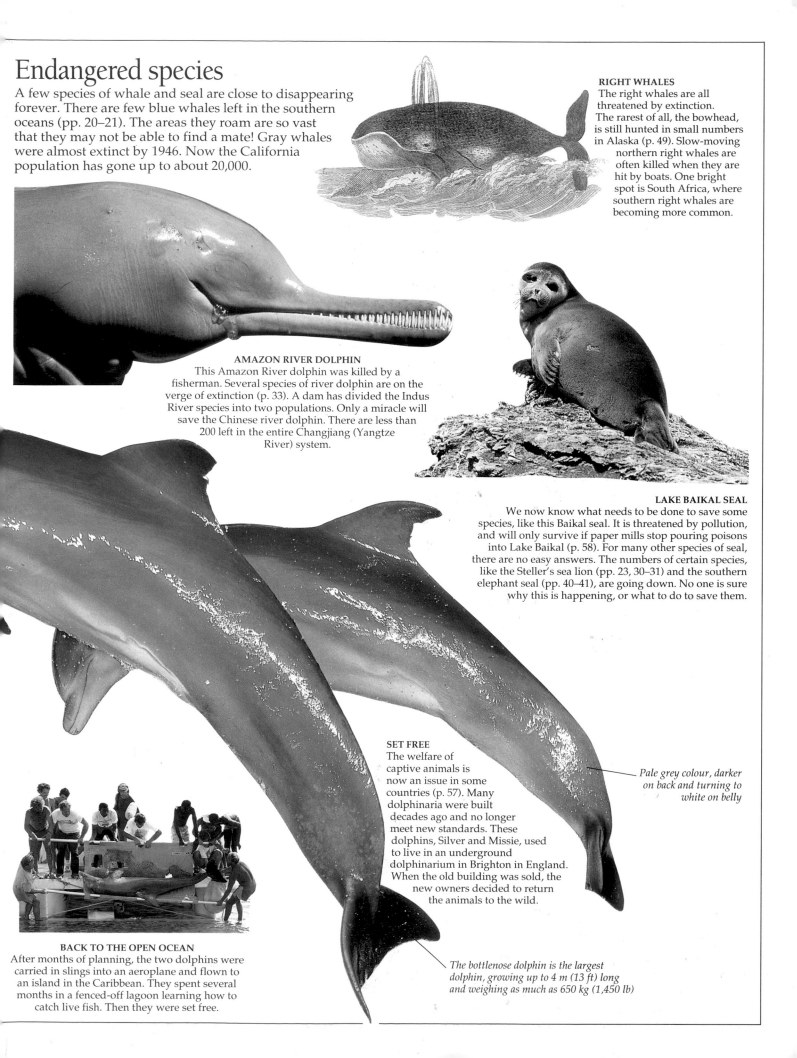

RIGHT WHALES
The right whales are all threatened by extinction. The rarest of all, the bowhead, is still hunted in small numbers in Alaska (p. 49). Slow-moving northern right whales are often killed when they are hit by boats. One bright spot is South Africa, where southern right whales are becoming more common.

AMAZON RIVER DOLPHIN
This Amazon River dolphin was killed by a fisherman. Several species of river dolphin are on the verge of extinction (p. 33). A dam has divided the Indus River species into two populations. Only a miracle will save the Chinese river dolphin. There are less than 200 left in the entire Changjiang (Yangtze River) system.

LAKE BAIKAL SEAL
We now know what needs to be done to save some species, like this Baikal seal. It is threatened by pollution, and will only survive if paper mills stop pouring poisons into Lake Baikal (p. 58). For many other species of seal, there are no easy answers. The numbers of certain species, like the Steller's sea lion (pp. 23, 30–31) and the southern elephant seal (pp. 40–41), are going down. No one is sure why this is happening, or what to do to save them.

SET FREE
The welfare of captive animals is now an issue in some countries (p. 57). Many dolphinaria were built decades ago and no longer meet new standards. These dolphins, Silver and Missie, used to live in an underground dolphinarium in Brighton in England. When the old building was sold, the new owners decided to return the animals to the wild.

Pale grey colour, darker on back and turning to white on belly

BACK TO THE OPEN OCEAN
After months of planning, the two dolphins were carried in slings into an aeroplane and flown to an island in the Caribbean. They spent several months in a fenced-off lagoon learning how to catch live fish. Then they were set free.

The bottlenose dolphin is the largest dolphin, growing up to 4 m (13 ft) long and weighing as much as 650 kg (1,450 lb)

Index

Acknowledgements

Vassili Papastavrou would like to dedicate this book to Catherine and thank Mel Brooks, Nigel & Jennifer Bonner, Tom Arnbom, Bill Amos, Denise Herzing, Graham Leach, Gill Hartley, Simon Hay and Nick Davies.
Dorling Kindersley would like to thank Jon Kershaw & the staff of Marineland, Antibes, France; Ron Kastelein & the staff of Harderwijk Marine Mammal Park, Holland; Adrian Friday & Ray Symonds at University Museum of Zoology, Cambridge, for skeletons (pp. 12, 13, 23, 25, 36, 40, 43); Bob Headland at Scott Polar Institute, Cambridge, for the harpoon gun (pp. 48–49) & Inuit sculptures (pp. 15, 42); John Ward at the British Antarctic Survey for the krill (p. 25); Arthur Credland at Town Docks Museum, Hull for the whaling artefacts (pp. 46–53); John Shearer for the nets (pp. 56–57); the Sea Mammal Research Unit, Cambridge, esp.

Christine Lockyer for the tooth (p. 60) & Kevin Nicholas & Bernie McConnell for the tags (p. 61); Sarah Richardson and the pupils of Townsend Primary School, London (p. 62); Jocelyn Steedman in Vancouver; Helena Spiteri for editorial help; Sharon Spencer, Manisha Patel and Jabu Mahlangu for design help.
Additional photography: Harry Taylor, Natural History Museum, London; Ivor Curzlake, British Museum, London (pp. 2–3, 33 & 54–55); Dave King (pp. 6, 10tl, 32–33 & 62–63) and Jerry Young (p. 7).
Index: Céline Carez

Picture credits

t=top b=bottom l=left r=right a=above c=centre
American Museum of Natural History, New York 20-21; Ancient Art & Architecture Collection 6tl, 36tl, 46tl; Aquarius Library / MGM 54cl; Ardea London Limited / F. Gohier 18tl, 56b; Tom Arnbom 41tl, 41tr; Auscape International / D. Parer & E. Parer-Cook 34cr, 34br; Baleine Blanche French School Afloat / G. Hartley 60c; Barnaby's Picture Library / W. Lüthy 48tl / N.D. Price 51cla; BFI / © Gaumont 1988 55bl; Bibliothèque Nationale, Paris / Gallimard Jeunesse 12bc; Nigel Bonner 48bl; Bridgeman Art Library / Giraudon 32tl/Private Collection 55tr, 57tl; Staatlich Antikens-ammlung, Munich 2tr; British Museum, London 42tr; Bruce Coleman Limited / Dr I. Everson 41cl / J. Foott 7bl, 35tr, 46br, 53b / F. Lanting 35cr / N. Lightfoot 53ca / D. & M. Plage 58b / Dr E. Potts 37cr / H. Reinhardt: 43tl; R. Ellis 62bl; E.T. Archive 53tc; Mary Evans Picture Library 32tr, 34tl, 36bl, 37tl, 42cl, 48br, 50tl, 55bl, 63tr; Werner Forman Archive / Field Museum of Natural History, USA 52cla; Greenpeace / Culley 49br / Gleizes 53cr / Martenson 59tl / Rowlands 59bl; © Hergé 9cr; Michael Holford 32bl, 56cl; I.F.A.W. 31cr; Jacana / F. Gohier 20cl, 21cr; Kendall Whaling Museum, Sharon ,Mass. , USA 50cl, 51clb; Frank Lane Picture Agency / T. Stephenson 63tl; Peter Lugárch 40cl; Mail Newspapers / Solo Syndication 63bl; Marineland / J. Foudraz 29cr, 29c; Minden Pictures / © F. Nicklin 39tr; Musée d'Histoire Naturelle, Paris / Gallimard Jeunesse 12bc; Natural History Museum, London 8tl, 9br, 10ca, 10cb, 20b, 36-37, 56cr; NHPA / B. & C.

Alexander 59tc / D. Currey 62tr/P. Johnson 29crb / T. Nakuniara 30cl; O.S.F / D. Allan 18cl, 25b, 37tr, 37cra, 49tl, 58tl, 58tr, 63cr / D. Fleetham 26bl / L.E. Lauber 28cl / T. Martin 49tr; Pacific Whale Foundation / © 1990 D. Moses 57br; V. Papastavrou 12tl, 38br; Planet Earth Pictures / J. King 38bl / Menuhin 18tr / F. Schulke 60tr / M. Snyderman 20cr, 33clb / J. D. Watt 6cl; Rex Features Limited / E. Thorburn 27tr / Roger-Viollet 21tr; Ann Ronan at Image Select 47tl, 48tr; Courtesy of the Royal British Columbia Museum ,Victoria, B.C. , Canada / B. Reid 54tr; Science Photo Library / European Space Agency 39tl; Sea Life Cruises / R. Fairbairns 17c; Sea Mammal Research Unit, Cambridge / Dr C. Lockyer 61bl; C. Hunter 61crb / Dr T Martin 56tl, 60cr, 62br; Service Historique de la Marine, Vincennes / Gallimard Jeunesse 6bl; Frank Spooner Pictures / Gamma 58cl; S. Steedman 57cl; Texas A & M University at Galveston / Dr B. Würsig 32br; Wild Dolphin Project Inc. / D. Herzing 29tl, 31tl.
Every effort has been made to trace the copyright holders and we apologise in advance for any unintentional omissions. We would be pleased to insert the appropriate acknowledgements in any subsequent edition of this publication.